PANDEMONIUM

A DISCORDANT CONCORDANCE

of

DIVERSE SPIRIT CATALOGUES

First published in 2016 by Hadean Press
West Yorkshire
Printed in England

HADEAN PRESS

www.hadeanpress.com

PANDEMONIUM

A Discordant Concordance

of

Diverse Spirit Catalogues

JAKE STRATTON-KENT

Students of the grimoires will be aware of the fluid, apparently arbitrary, way in which hierarchies come down to us.

Peter Grey, *Lucifer: Princeps*

CONTENTS

Contents

ACKNOWLEDGEMENTS

Joseph H. Peterson for all his work and sharing.
Mallorie Vaudoise for her translation of *Le Livre des Esperitz*.
Kevin Heinrich for generous technical assistance.
Brendan Hughes for various major favours and his time.
Brian Henderson for remote maintenance.
Aristomenes Christos Papageorgopolous for shared scholarship.
Innumerable friends and readers for encouragement and feedback.

PREFACE

READIER ACCESS to a larger and more representative portion of the grimoire genre in recent years has had some remarkable results. Among these has been a re-examination of the formerly pre-eminent *Goetia of Solomon*. The 'default' reliance on the spirits of the *Goetia*, their arrangement, ranking and number – even the spelling of their names – no longer holds. Some lessons in this direction had already been established regarding its partial dependence on Scot's *Discoverie of Witchcraft* and its rendition of Weyer's spirit catalogue, the *Pseudomonarchia daemonum*. Among the points in this regard were that both Scot and the *Goetia of Solomon* omit Pruslas, a spirit from Weyer's list. Also, the *Goetia of Solomon* adds spirits not found in Weyer. In my opinion many of these additions reflect English traditions, for example Andromalius is identical with 'Andrew Malchus' (sic) a spirit known from English trial records.

Another emergent consideration in comparative work is that 'reliability' regarding the spirit catalogue is not completely dependent on date or the perceived respectability of a given text. It is not difficult to demonstrate that the editors of the despised blue genre had access to better manuscript sources than those to which they are sometimes unfavourably compared. In relation to the spirit catalogue specifically, *Wellcome MS 4669* completely omits the powers of four major spirits it shares with *The Grimorium Verum*, while the account of them in *Verum* itself is far more complete. As it turns out, two of these particular spirits are important links between a greater variety of sources, printed and manuscript. *Verum* cannot have derived its account of them from either of the two manuscripts supposed to have 'preceded' it. At the time of writing Joseph Peterson is preparing an edition of a superior previously unknown source, which I await with interest. That the GV had excellent sources and represents an authentic tradition really should not be surprising.

So too, earlier continental grimoires such as the *Livre des Esperitz* represent a tradition in many ways distinct from evolving English forms such as the *Goetia of Solomon*. Since the spirit catalogues were not derived from the *Goetia*, they are also not supportive of its assumptions about the spirit hierarchy. Later on, of course, the French had as much access to Weyer as did the English. The appearance of eighteen of Weyer's spirits in the *Grand Grimoire*, including the very one omitted by both Scot and the *Goetia*, is only one indicator of this. Too much precedence has often been given to known manuscripts – often in British collections – over similar material in the 'late grimoires' with their own sources. Often too little attention has been placed on the quality of given parts of the blue grimoires. This applies in particular to the spirit catalogues, where the earliest known printed editions are often superior to supposed 'predecessor' mss. An element of favouritism occasionally intrudes when considering these grimoires, and lack of impartiality. Informed opinion has long been aware there are gaps in the literary record, and allowances for this require less selective application forthwith.

Abbreviations Used

AG   *The Grimoire of Arthur Gauntlet*. David Rankine (ed). Avalonia. 2011.

BTS   *The Book of Treasure Spirits*. David Rankine (ed). Avalonia. 2009.

CBM   *The Cambridge Book of Magic*. Francis Young (trans). Cambridge. 2015.

CGP   *The Complete Grimoire of Pope Honorius*. David Rankine and Paul Harry Barron (eds). Avalonia. 2013.

FR   *Forbidden Rites, a Necromancer's Manual of the Fifteenth Century*. Richard Kieckhefer. Pennsylvania State University Press. 1997.

GG   *The Grand Grimoire*

GH   *The Grimoire of Pope Honorius*

GoS   *The Goetia of Solomon*

GV   *The Grimorium Verum*

JHP   Joseph H. Peterson

KGM   *The Keys to the Gateway of Magic*. Steve Skinner and David Rankine (eds). Golden Hoard. Singapore. 2011.

LBA   Lucifer – Belzebuth – Astaroth

LBS   Lucifer – Belzebuth – Satan

LdE   *Le Livre des Esperitz*

Lec   Claude Lecouteux. *Le Livre Grimoires*. Imago. Paris. 2008.

LKS   *The Lesser Key of Solomon*. Joseph H. Peterson (ed). Weiser. York Beach USA. 2001.

MTS   *The Magical Treatise of Solomon, or Hygromanteia*. Ioannis Marakathis (ed).

Off   *A Book of the Offices of Spirits*. Colin D. Campbell (ed). Teitan Press. 2011. [also contained in: Daniel Harms, James R. Clark and Joseph H. Peterson, *The Book of Oberon*. Llewellyn. 2015.]

PGM   *Papyri Graecae Magicae*, (Greek Magical Papyri).

Scot   Reginald Scot. *The Discoverie of Witchcraft* (various editions).

TCM   *The Testament of Cyprian the Mage*. Jake Stratton-Kent. Scarlet Imprint. 2014.

TG   *The True Grimoire*. Jake Stratton-Kent (ed). Scarlet Imprint. 2010.

ToS   *Testament of Solomon*

Weyer   Johann Weyer aka Johann Weirus aka Johann Weir. *Pseudomonarchia Daemonum*.

VKS   *The Veritable Keys of Solomon*. Steve Skinner and David Rankine, (eds). Llewellyn. Minnesota USA. 2008.

Le Livre des Esperitz
THE BOOK OF SPIRITS

HERE BEGINS the *Book of Spirits,* the one which was revealed to the sage Solomon to constrain them on earth and make them obey human will, for before the science was found, shown, manifested, and revealed to Solomon, the spirits made too many evils and pestilences on earth and destroyed many good things in this world, and upon the human line made various persecutions; and God in his mercy gave to Solomon the benefit of this holy science to constrain the spirits that they might obey human creatures, and their malice would not reign anymore over the Christian earth.

At the beginning of the book are placed the names of the spirits who are governors and masters of all the other spirits; of the region and office of Lucifer; of the office of Bezlebut; of Satan; of the four spirits who are Governors of the four regions and parts of the world, that is to know of the spirit who is called Orient, of Poymon, of Equi; of Veal, the great king; of Agarat, duke; of Barbas, prince; of Bulfas, prince; of Amon, marquis; of Batal, count; of Gemen, king; of Gazon, duke; of Artis, prince; of Machin, duke; of Dicision, king; of Abugor, duke; of Vipos, count; of Cerbere, marquis; of Carmola, prince; of Estor, duke; of Coap, prince; of Deas, duke; of Asmoday, king; of Bitur, marquis; of Beal, duke; of Forcas, prince; of Furfur, count; of Margotias, marquis; of Oze, prince; of Lucay, marquis; of Pucel, duke; of Jayn, count; of Suralet, duke; of Zagon, king; of Dragon, prince; of Parcas, prince; of Gorsin, duke; of Andralfas, marquis; of Flanos, duke; of Brial, king; of Fenix, marquis; of Distolas.

[1] *Lucifer* was very beautiful and of such stature, as were the other good angels, and did not stay placed in the skies for the space of one hour, for he became proud by watching and contemplating the great beauty in which he was formed; and all those who were plotting evil with him were thrown into Hell in confusion. In fact Lucifer, according to what the doctors of nigromancy say, presides in Hell and all the aforementioned spirits of Hell obey him as the sovereign of Hell.

[2] Licentious, great and evil spirit, is called *Bezlebuth*, and was called before the Time of Solomon Anthaon, and is the Greatest of Hell after Lucifer, and one must know that he rules the eastern places, and he who calls him must keep his face towards east and he will appear to him in beautiful face and semblance. He teaches all sciences and gives gold and silver to those that constrain him to come, and gives true response to that which one asks of him, and reveals the secrets of Hell if one asks him, and teaches truly the hidden things in earth and in the sea, and so manifests all treasures which are resting in earth, and guards the other spirits, and must be called in good weather.

[3] *The third spirit is called Satan*, that one which was formed after Lucifer, and speaks in the air near us. Sathan appears in gracious semblance and lives in the North. He who calls him must have his face towards the North, He appears and his power is to transform all men and women if one commands him, and appears to do all evils if he is commanded.

Of the four principle spirits are said the offices in this part, of which the first follows:

Sequitur de primo
The first is called Orient and lives in the East. He holds the name of that part of the world.

Pro secundo
The second is called Poymon and lives in the West.

Pro tertio
The third is called Amoymon and lives in southern parts.

Pro quarto
The fourth is called Equi and lives in the northern parts.

[4] Officium primi
The office of the first who is called Orient, is to answer truly to that which one asks him, and has power to gather all spirits and command their actions, and teaching the master that constrains him all physicke [medicine etc]; and beneath him are 100 legions of angels or evil spirits.

[5] Poymon
Poymon appears in the semblance of a crowned woman, very resplendent, and rides a camel. He who constrains him must have his face towards the west, and he answers truly of what one asks him, and teaches all sciences to the master, and manifests all hidden things, and gives dignities and great lordships, and makes all malicious works of the master come to mercy plainly; and is lord of 25 legions.

[6] Aymoymon
Aymoymon is a king and appears in semblance of a half-man with a long beard, and wears on his head a very clear crown, and loves when one makes him a sacrifice, and gives true response to that which you ask him or concede, and gives memory of all sciences and gives great dignities on earth and confirms them, and gives good manner of good sense; and has 10 legions.

[Equi omitted]

[7] Beal

Beal is a great king who is beneath and is subject to Orient, who is great and makes man marvellously invisible, and gives his grace to all things; and under him are 6 legions.

[8] Agarat

Agarat is a duke and appears benignly in the semblance of an old man and teaches all languages and gives lordships and great dignities on earth; and under him are 36 legions.

[9] Barthas

Barthas is a great prince who appears with a beautiful face. His office is to give response to that which one asks of him, and teach hidden things, and also teaches and do to or for people whatever one asks him, and turns men into whatever shape the master wants, and teaches astronomy perfectly; and under him are 36 legions.

[10] Bulfas

Bulfas is a great prince. His office is to make discords and battles, and when he is well constrained, he returns good responses to whatever one asks him; and beneath him are 36 legions.

[11] Amon

Amon is a great marquis who appears in the semblance of a virgin. His office is to speak truth of things past and to come upon Earth, and every person whose love one wants to have, he gives it; and has under him 40 legions.

[12] Barbas

Barbas is a prince who shows how to understand the voices of birds and of dogs, and manifests all things hidden within the earth, and carries them if one commands him; and he has 36 legions.

Pandemonium: A Discordant Concordance of Diverse Spirit Catalogues

[13] Gemer

Gemer is a great king. His office is to teach the virtue of herbs and all sciences, and cure those who are sick when one commands him, and also make people sick; and beneath him he has 40 legions.

[14] Gazon

Gazon is a great duke who gives true response to things past, future and present, and gives grace and love of all people upon earth, and makes one rise in great honours and dignities; and has 40 legions.

[15] Artis

Artis is a great duke and has two crowns, and a sword in his hand. His office is to respond to all things that one wants to ask of him and to teach hidden things, and gives good love and grace between any persons; and has 36 legions.

[16] Machin

Machin is a great duke in similitude and semblance of a strong man, and teaches the virtue of herbs and precious stones, and brings the master from region to region wherever the master desires; and has 37 legions.

[17] Diusion

Diusion is a great king who appears in the semblance of a handsome man, and gives true response to what one asks of him, and seeks out treasures hidden in the earth when one commands him; and has 24 legions.

[18] Abugor

Abugor is a great duke who appears in the semblance of a handsome knight, and gives true answers of what one asks him, and of things hidden in the earth, and gives good grace of kings and other lords; and has 27 legions.

[19] Vipos
Vipos is a great count who appears in the semblance of an angel, and makes man wise and hardy, and speaks truth of that which one asks him; and has 25 legions.

[20] Cerbere
Cerbere is a great marquis who gives perfect understanding in all sciences and makes man very great in honours and riches; and has 19 legions.

[21] Carmola
Carmola is a great prince who gives understanding of birds and of trapping thieves and murderers when one commands him. He makes people invisible and speaks truth of that which one asks; and has 26 legions.

[22] Salmatis
Salmatis is a great marquis who appears in the semblance of an armed knight, and makes man appear in whatever semblance he wants, and constructs fortresses, buildings, castles and cities when one commands him, and makes great wounds appear on whatever person; and has 50 legions.

[23] Coap
Coap is a great prince who gives use of women and brings them where one wants and makes them beside themselves if one commands him; he has 27 legions.

[24] Drap
Drap is a great duke who speaks basely and harms sight and hearing when one commands him; and has IIIIxx [sic] legions.

[25] Asmoday
Asmoday is a great king who gives a ring of great virtue that makes whoever wears it prosper in all worldly things, and he

gives true answer to what one asks him; and has under him 12 legions.

[26] Caap

Caap is a great prince who appears in the form of a knight and answers truly what one asks him, and brings gold and silver from whatever place one commands him; and has under him 20 legions.

[27] Bune

Bune is a great duke who directs bodies to and from one place to another, and makes men rich and speak eloquently in front of all people, and gives true answers to what one asks of him; and has 35 legions.

[28] Bitur

Bitur is a great marquis who appears in the form of a beautiful young man and gives the love of women from whatever place they may be, and destroys cities and castles if the master commands him, and removes great worldly honours and dignities if the master commands him; and has 36 legions.

[29] Lucubar

Lucubar is a great duke who makes man subtle and full of great ingenuity, and transforms lead into gold and pewter into silver, in what ever manner one desires. [Legions omitted]

[30] Bugan

Bugan is a great king who makes man wise and transforms all types of metal into any other as you wish, and water into wine or into oil; and has 34 legions.

[31] Parcas

Parcas is a great prince who makes men subtle. He appears in a beautiful form. He knows the virtue of herbs and precious stones and brings them when one commands him, and makes man invisible and wise in all sciences, and makes man become young or old, whichever one wants, and makes sight recover when one has lost it. And he brings gold and silver that is hidden in the earth and all other things, and carries the master throughout all the world if one commands him, and all other persons if the master commands him; and has under him 30 legions.

[32] Flavos

Flavos is a great duke who gives true answer to what one asks of him, and destroys all adversaries of the master who constrains him; and has 20 legions.

[33] Vaal

Vaal is a great king who gives true answers of all in this world, and gives lordships, dignities, good grace to people, and disperses it as one commands him; and has 49 legions.

[34] Fenix

Fenix is a great marquis who appears in beautiful form, and has a sweet soft voice, and he is courteous and very obedient of all one wants to ask him about or command him to do, and he does them without dallying; and has 25 legions.

[35] Distolas

Distolas is a great marquis who appears in beautiful form and responds willingly to what one asks and commands him, and he bring stones if one commands him, and gives the master a horse who carries him in one hour 100 or 200 or 300 leagues or more; and has 20 legions.

[36] Berteth

Berteth is a great duke who appears in beautiful form and has a crown. He gives answers truly to what one asks him, and he teaches how to convert all types of metal into gold or silver, and gives lordships and confirms them if one asks him; and has 26 legions.

[37] Dam
Dam is a great count who appears in beautiful form, he brings gold and silver and all other things if one commands him, and makes all persons who one commands him to die or languish. And he tells all the secrets of women, and he makes them disrobe and dance completely naked; and has 25 legions.

[38] Furfur
Furfur is a great count who appears in the guise of an angel and grants the love of all people, and makes men wise in astronomy and philosophy. [Legions omitted]

[39] Forcas
Forcas is a great prince who teaches the virtue of herbs and precious stones, and makes one become invisible and wise and eloquent to all people, and he brings treasures hidden in the earth when one commands him; and has 30 legions.

[40] Malpharas
Malpharas is a great lord who constructs towers and castles, bridges on bodies of water when one commands him, and attacks and confounds people, castles or other fortresses, and carries from one place to another as one commands him, and obeys and is courteous to the master who thus constrains him; and has 30 legions.

[41] Gorsay
Gorsay is a great duke who makes a man able in works and speech. He takes thieves and murderers wherever one commands him to, and makes whoever one wants suffer pain and torment; and has 15 legions.

[42] Samon
Samon is a great king who appears in the semblance of a beautiful virgin. He answers what one asks him about. He teaches of goods and treasures which are hidden and perfectly

grants the love of all queens and women, be they virgins or not; and has 25 legions.

[43] Tudiras Hoho

Tudiras Hoho is a great marquis who appears in the semblance of a beautiful virgin and makes man wise in all sciences, and he turns him into a bird; and has 31 legions.

[44] Oze

Oze is a great marquis who answers truly what one asks of him, and he turns a man from one form to another, and he makes things appear like what they are not, and he makes a strand of straw be a great horse and a straw be a belt of gold or silver, and makes men mad when one commands him; and has 25 legions.

[45] Ducay

Ducay is a great marquis who appears very benignly and gives the love of women and makes all languages understood, and carries from one place to another; and has 25 legions.

[46] Bucal

Bucal is a great duke who appears in the guise of an angel and gives true answer to what one asks him, and makes great waters and abysses appear in the air, even though they aren't really there; and has 28 legions.

Finis.
Laudat opus.
Adsit in principio sancta Maria meo.

INTRODUCTION

THIS IS A BOOK about grimoire spirits, and the main view at all times is to clarify the important personalities, their roles and inter-relations, rather than simply focus on relevant historical texts with their dates, authors and impedimenta. To achieve these goals, various technical aspects will only be detailed as sub-topics. These digressions will be interrupted frequently by 'spirit biographies' to keep on track. It's quite dense stuff; be prepared to make more than one pass.

While trying to steer away from the books, somehow or other though, their aesthetic remains useful in talking about the spirits concerned. Hence, many tables. The first table compresses into a contained visual form the various aspects of a large submerged territory to be explored in these chapters. It will be the first of many tables and precedes various discussions of convergent and divergent subjects. It is a table about books, to introduce many tables about spirits. The connecting element with these books and various others to be discussed is the *dramatis personæ*, which exist independently, at least in inter- and extra-textual form, and require a discussion unto themselves.

SPIRIT HIERARCHY OVERVIEW

	Livre de Esperitz	Folger Book of Offices and English stemma	Weyer (Pseudo-monarchia Daemonorum); Scot's Discoverie of Witchcraft; Goetia of Solomon	Honorius	Clavicle*, Grimorium Verum, Grand Grimoire
Trinity of Lucifer, Belzebuth Satan (and/or Astaroth)	Yes	Yes	No, likely beginning with deliberate omission	Explicit	Yes
Four Kings	Explicit	Explicit	Confused and contra-dictory	Explicit	Variant
Presidential Council	Implicit	Explicit	Implicit	Variant	Variant
Sub Kings or Messengers	Implicit	Yes	Implicit	No or variant	Variant
Catalogue of Spirits	Yes	Yes	Yes	No	Variant

*Wellcome MS 4669 and Lansdowne MS 1202 Livre Troiseme include differing variant forms of the Verum catalogue with peculiar variants in the names of subordinate spirits. These ms versions precede the first Bibliotheque Bleue printing of the Grimorium Verum, and have been assumed to be prototypes. However, the names of subordinate spirits as given in Verum rather than the mss have earlier precedents in continental traditions. These indicate that the text deserves at least equal weight with the mss. French sources of the C19th invariably do not distinguish the GV from the Clavicle, and numerous academic works follow this more accurate precedent.

LUCIFER, BELZEBUTH, AND SATAN

As HAS BEEN SEEN, the *Livre des Esperitz* begins its catalogue with Lucifer, Belzebuth and Satan, moving on to the Four Kings and then a catalogue of spirits. This is now widely recognised as the structure implicit behind the Weyer catalogue and *Goetia* as well as explicit in other related grimoires of the same family. It is spelled out in longer form in the *Book of Offices* (either Hockley's transcription or directly from the *Book of Oberon*), and imitated in various works by Doctor Rudd and his school. It is therefore only right that our account of the grimoire spirits begins with them.

The opening part of the *Book of Offices* follows a similar pattern to the *LdE*, with an account of the three Chiefs and the four Kings. While the text is more elaborated the same inspiration can be detected readily. Lucifer is termed the father of all devils, as Belzebuth is their Prince. The former may not be called, but spirits can be conjured and bound in his name; for that 'all devils do reverence and worship' him and 'with a kind of majesty' obey him.

The *Book of Offices* is perhaps more reliable than *LdE* regarding the name of the god under which Belzebuth was worshipped. It names Hades' ancient ferryman, Charon, still known as a devil in Greek folklore. Among many points of accordance, the two texts agree that Belzebuth may be called, and, specifically, toward the East. This requirement should not be confused with the role of the King(s) of the East, which has a much more general relevance. East is simply the place of power *par excellence*, as will be seen.

Satan is perhaps the most controversial figure to appear in the newly emergent picture of grimoire 'orthodoxy'. It is certainly important to understand him in the proper context, the magico-mythical one. Created immediately after Lucifer, and dwelling and heard in the air (*LdE*), he is the 'prince of the powers of the air' beloved of demonologists. He abideth in an obscure air (or obscurely in the air: *Off*; *Sloane 3824*), distinctly reminiscent of the Headless One (as per various renderings of PGM.V.121). Further, the Four Kings, who are chiefs of aerial spirits, are known to and obey him (*Off*). Give or take some differences in spelling, these are: Oriens, Paymon, Amaymon and Egyn. Satan's old title of 'Prince of the Powers of the Air' carries this connotation implicitly.

It should be noted that Lucifer is not to be called, Belzebuth may be – and that on rare occasions rather than as part of regular practice – while Satan's governance is subdivided in relation to the quarters. Among the Four Kings of the quarters, Oriens, King of the East, is traditionally deemed superior in authority to the other three. This underlines that Belzebuth is not here seen as a 'King' of the East, but that the East has special dignity throughout the underlying conception.

That all the sections dealing with these three spirits and the Four Kings are of greater length in *Offices* than most of its other spirits, invites comparison with the Long Text group in Weyer. While in *LdE* these sections appear in the same order but no longer than the others, by far the longest spirit section in the whole work belongs to Partas. This is a subject to which it will be necessary to return.

Regarding the so called LBS and LBA trinities, on the face of it the various versions of the *Grimoire of Pope Honorius* represents the latter. In at least one of its forms the spirits of the first three days of the week are Lucifer, Belzebuth, and Astaroth. In fact, classing it along with the *Grand* and the *True* grimoires is certainly not out of place. However, the spirit of Saturday is conjured 'in the name of Satan and of Belzebuth, in the name of Astarot and of all the other spirits'. This is our first clue that the trinities are not so exclusive, and may point to *Honorius* – or its sources – as an important link in our understanding. Said grimoire also contains invocations of the Four Kings, though in a variant form.

Having already discussed the Four Kings in great detail in *TCM*, it is useful to consider the greater Chiefs and their associates as presented by *Honorius*. This serves various purposes by illustrating that presenting key features of the spirit hierarchy is not reliant on any particular grimoire. At the same time some relevant and under-examined aspects of *The Grimoire of Pope Honorius* can be highlighted relatively seamlessly.

THE SPIRITS OF THE SEVEN DAYS

IN THE *Grimoire of Pope Honorius* (*GH* or *Honorius*) and some editions of the *True Grimoire* (*GV* or *Verum*) appear seven invocations of spirits attributed to the weekdays. The various editions of *Honorius* approach this in slightly different ways, while sharing common features. The approach as it appears in the Italian editions of *Verum* - working within its own ritual structures - is usefully independent of other aspects of the *Honorius* system.

There are differences among these grimoires over which spirit is attributed, with some consistent cases. There are resolvable variations in the hours specified as appropriate. Other differences are to be found in conjurations employed and the circles for each day; these are technicalities largely of concern to other interests. Mine concern the spirits themselves and, for the present, the model of time involved in the attribution. My sympathies, it should be clear, do not reside with the exorcists of the clerical underground. My preference for *Verum* over *Honorius* as regards method relates directly to these sympathies.

THE SPIRITS OF THE DAYS OF THE WEEK,
ACCORDING TO *VERUM* AND *HONORIUS*

	Monday	Tuesday	Wednesday	Thursday	Friday	Saturday	Sunday
Honorius 1800	Lucifer	Nambroth	Astaroth	Acham	Bechet	Nabam	Aquiel
Honorius 1760	Lucifer	Frimost	Astaroth	Silchade	Bechard	Guland	Surgat
Honorius 1670	Trinitas*	Nambrot	Astaroth	Acham	Bechet	Nebirots	Acquiot
Italian Verum	Lucifer	Belzebuth	Astaroth	Silchade	Bechard	Guland	Surgat

*Trinitas is the name attached to the Circle; the conjuration is addressed to Lucifer.

One important common feature among these variants is that the attribution of the weekdays consistently begins with Monday rather than Sunday. The only exception is a late German variant, where the spirit of Sunday has obviously been moved to the beginning. 'Faustian' influences rather than Solomonic orthodoxy probably explain this adaptation, but it is the Monday start principle that requires our attention.

It is to be contrasted with, for example, the week beginning with Sunday 'ruled' by Michael, leader of the angels. This is the 'norm' embodied by the *Heptameron*, and implicit in the majority of Solomonic grimoires in their planetary associations and so forth. In these systems not only does the Sun – or its angel – rule the day, its first hour and so on, but is implicitly or explicitly considered 'leader' of the week (as represented by other angels and spirits of days and hours).

The conception here implies that the beginning of the 'demonic' week is the day of the nocturnal Moon, rather than the diurnal Sun. Similarly, the hours given for conjuration in every case are hours of the night. This double nocturnal emphasis is unusual and significant.

HOURS OF WORKING

Monday	Lucifer (Trinitas)	Between 11th and 12th hours.	or the 3rd and 4th hours of the night.
Tuesday	Belzebuth. Frimost or Nambroth.	Between 9th and 10th hours of the night.	
Wednesday	Astaroth	Between 10th and 11th hours of the night.	
Thursday	Acham or Silcharde	Between 3rd and 4th hours of the night.	
Friday	Bechard	Between 11th and 12th hours of the night.	
Saturday	Nabam (Nambroth). Nebirots. Guland	[Between 3rd and 4th or 10th and 11th hours of the night.]	[times not given in text]
Sunday	Aquiel or Surgat	Between 10th and 11th hours of the night.	

Possibly these were originally all 3rd and 4th and 10th and 11th, as these are the appropriate 'planetary hours' of the night of each planetary day in every case. It is, in any case, radically different from the largely diurnal timings as initially given by Weyer and modified in the *Goetia*.

The week of Honorius and the 'sublunary worlds'

> But magic, according to the Greeks, is a thing of a very powerful nature. For they say that this forms the last part of the sacerdotal science. Magic, indeed, investigates the nature, power, and quality of everything sublunary; viz. of the elements, and their parts, of animals, all various plants and their fruits, of stones and herbs: and in short, it explores the essence and power of every thing. From hence, therefore, it produces its effects.
>
> Michael Psellus:
> *On Daemons according to the Dogmas of the Greeks.*

If we map the weekday attributions as they appear in *Honorius* as a linear model it presents a striking resemblance to part of the old Neoplatonist cosmology. Thus it begins with the sphere of the moon, descending to the aerial sphere divided into four elemental parts, with the terrestrial and subterrene or infernal region below them. As Psellus observes, all magical endeavour and occult science is concerned with the sublunar sphere. This sphere is also the realm of all grimoire spirits in accordance with Christian theology beginning with St. Augustine, preceded by Neoplatonist and Chaldean thought, all drawing on more archaic themes and models. In the models of Late Antiquity – from which we receive the week beginning with Sunday, unlike the Jewish week – the sublunar sphere was the realm of the elements. This is the background from which is derived the conception of aerial spirits associated with the four elements.

ILLUSTRATION OF THE ARISTOTELIAN UNIVERSE FROM PETER APIANUS'S
COSMOGRAPHICUM LIBER, 1533.

THE SUBLUNAR SPHERES

Pandemonium: A Discordant Concordance of Diverse Spirit Catalogues

In this conception there were seven planetary spheres above while the sublunar realm contained four, one for each element. Given the directional associations of the elements and their rulers we should probably not take this too literally. It should also be borne carefully in mind that the planets were latecomers to the mythic language, while the transcendental 'source' is even later. Thus the sublunar part of this model actually reprises older traditions, with additional layers merely superimposed by later philosophy. These I propose we delete, retaining the sublunar model alone without the transcendentalist veneer. The planetary attributions of the days are worth retaining, but should be viewed as suggestive rather than restrictive. In particular, viewing the sublunar region as a reflection of the planets should be avoided. While later philosophers may well have viewed things this way, historically the features of the sublunar realm preceded planetary classifications; if anything the planets reflect the features of the 'lower' world. Similarly, elemental classifications of the days and the levels they represent are useful in the first analysis, but are also capable of contradiction.

In Orphic and Theurgic systems are embedded echoes of older traditions relevant today – envisaging Sun and Moon as the Isles of Hades and Persephone respectively, for example. Clearly associating Hades with the Sun makes sense within this modelling. That Persephone is traditionally close to or synonymous with Hecate also adds all manner of important nuances. For example, our Four Elements (with their Kings, ministers and spirits) are often answerable to Satan in traditional grimoire lore, while in traditions of Late Antiquity Hecate (Astaroth) has identical authority over spirits, elementals, and ghosts in the aerial region. The interplay between LBS and LBA trinities makes a good deal more sense when this is borne in mind.

The Honorian model then, while measuring Time, also refers to physical space or its mythic counterparts. The schema is not planetary as such, but sub-lunar with distinctly secondary planetary attributions. In fact, it is important not to understand spirits within this schema as planetary; in Neoplatonist terms the planetary worlds are 'reflected' in the sublunar world. As older levels of mythological understanding are involved in this model, this supposed correspondence with hypothetical 'higher worlds' is suggestive rather than definitive. Similarly, traditional attribution to the elements within this model is also subordinate to the older and more fundamental concept of directionality.

With these provisos, the first of the seven layers of the model refers to the Moon. The four subsequent refer to the four directions; while often seen as elemental they are more essentially concerned with directional divisions among the aerial spirits. The last two levels refer to spirits 'upon the Earth and under the Earth' (both distinct from elemental earth as such). The Underworld Sun (as distinct from the diurnal Sun) is thus the seventh and last.

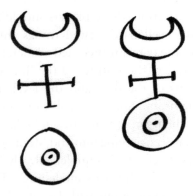

NOCTURNAL COSMOLOGY

The essentials of this model are ancient, but better known in more recent guises which are more readily assimilated. The sublunar region as understood in late Antiquity was seen as the world of the Elements. Expecting distinct elemental qualities among aerial spirits of different directions is overly simplistic. However, the subterranean Sun points to a more organic perception of sublunar elements, mirroring the description of the elementals in the *True Grimoire*:

> In the first part is taught the means of calling forth the Elemental Spirits of the Air, Earth, Sea and Infernus, according to the correct correspondences.

The placing of Fire as 'lowest' in the above quotation should be read in accordance with the conception of the Midnight Sun in the model.

Day of the Week	'Planet'	Spirit Type	Named Spirits
Monday	Moon	Superiors	Lucifer, Trinitas
Tuesday	Mars	Northern, aquatic	Frimost aka Nambroth
Wednesday	Mercury	Western, aerial	Astaroth
Thursday	Jupiter	Eastern, fiery	Sirchade
Friday	Venus	Southern, earthy	Bechet or Bechaud
Saturday	Saturn	Terrestrial	Nebiros
Sunday	Sun	Subterranean	Aciel (aka Aquiot, Aquiel, Azael)

With this framework in mind we are then able to move forward through the first layer of the historical data, the seven-day schema as represented in *Honorius*.

MONDAY – LUCIFER/TRINITAS

Monday as the first day of the lunar week is that of Lucifer, the Emperor of spirits, their pre-eminent chief. The association of Lucifer with this day implies the rulership of the Moon as a ruler of Time. The hours employed are also of the night. The contrast of these operating principles with the usual solar emphasis is strongly reminiscent of the concept of 'sects' in astrology, whereby the Moon rules the nocturnal sect, and the Sun the diurnal. The concept of the Moon as ruler of the week (or of a cycle of time, four weeks to a lunar month and so forth) also suggests sympathies with lunar mansions rather than solar decans. These implications suggest depths and potentials within this approach distinguishing it from more familiar and pedestrian methods.

The association of the conjuration for Monday with 'Trinitas' is also replete with implications. In the hierarchy of the *Verum* system are three chiefs, all present in various *Honorius* texts. These are, namely, Lucifer, Belzebuth, and Astaroth. Belzebuth is not always attributed to a day, although in the syncretic *Wellcome* MS his *Verum* conjuration is given immediately before the discussion of the weekdays. There are three distinct conjurations for the chiefs in the *Verum* system, which in Italian editions also appear in the *Verum* account of the week. The *Wellcome* redaction of *Honorius*, where all three chiefs are present, also demonstrates familiarity with these conjurations and other aspects of the GV. At the same time, the word Trinitas at least implies a concept of all three chiefs in one, either as present or to become so in some manner as yet mysterious.

A similarly mysterious concept is found in Kimbanda, in the relations of the 'Maioral' to the Exu parallels of our chiefs (Exu Lucifer, Exu Mors, and Exu Rei De Sete Encruzilhadas respectively). Trinitas, then, is the pre-eminent singular form arising from the three chiefs. While lunar and nocturnal the Trinitas resembles the Maioral of Kimbanda, which embodies features of ancient solar pantheism. It follows that while all three chiefs may be adored and invoked on this day, all direct operations involve the Emperor Lucifer. The Emperor of spirits is the ultimate authority among them. His appearances are a rare mark of favour; he is not conjured so much as invoked. Nevertheless, it is not inappropriate to make offerings and ask marks of favour of him on Mondays. His invocation may also precede works with his deputies and their subordinates. Two deputies of Lucifer appear in various guises in numerous Solomonic MSS, as also the *True* and the *Grand* grimoires, and the books of Cyprian.

The subordinates of these two spirits require careful differentiation. Firstly, there are the sets of three attributed to them in the primary listing of the *True Grimoire*. There Satanachia rules Claunech, Musisin and Bechaud; Agliarept rules Frimost, Klepoth and Khil. Bechaud and Frimost are of course among the spirits of the Seven Days. There are also the spirits associated with them in the *Grand Grimoire*, also found in *Cyprian*, and derived from the same listing (most likely Weyer, and clearly independent of the *Goetia*). Therein Satanachia rules Pruslas, Amon and Barbatos; Agliarept rules Buer, Guyson and Botis.

Finally, there are spirits from the secondary listing of the *True Grimoire* and its mss variants. These spirits and their inter-relations with various deputies are named together in a major *Verum* conjuration. In this context Satanachia rules Serguthy, Heramael, Trimasael and Sustugriel, while Agliarept is a co-ruler of Elelogap. Nebiros is also named in the same conjuration, further connecting this listing with the Seven Days theme and with spell work.

TUESDAY – BELZEBUTH, OR FRIMOST, NAMBROTH

As Prince of the hierarchy Belzebuth is second only to Lucifer in rank and authority. He is a most dangerous spirit, particular about procedure and unforgiving of lapses. As a great spirit he is not, usually, appropriate for conjuration, but rather invoked as an authority in operations concerning his deputies and their subordinates.

The deputies of Belzebuth in the *True Grimoire* are Tarchimache (aka Tarihimal) and Flerity. The first of these also appears in the collective conjuration mentioned previously. Their subordinates are Mersilde, Clisthert, and Sirchade for Tarchimache, Hiepacth, Humots, and Segal for Flerity. Here again, Sirchade is also numbered among the spirits of the seven days.

In the *Grand Grimoire* Lucifuge Rofocale takes the place of Tarchimache, and rules Baal, Agares, and Marbas, while Flerity rules Bathim, Pursan, and Eligor. Tarihimal is co-ruler of Elelogap in the spell-related secondary listing of the *True Grimoire*, who also appears in the collective conjuration.

Frimost is a subordinate of Agliarept and a most important spirit. His sigil is written upon the wand of evocation in the method of the *Grimorium Verum*. This represents his power and authority, and his unique role among the spirits is similarly shown by his being sole possessor of the rank of Baron, as will be shown below. He shares many qualities with Belzebuth, but is far more approachable. Thus he mediates some powers of the Prince in operations of this day.

Tuesday is associated with various spirit names, some of which may be taken as aliases. Nambroth is associated with Tuesday in more than one version of *Honorius*, of which *Wellcome MS 4666* deserves and repays attention. Alternatively, Frimost is conjured on Tuesday in the Italian *Verum* and in *Honorius* 1760. Nambroth, who has other aliases and identities, may be taken as synonymous with Frimost, an identity with important aspects to be discussed anon. That he 'substitutes' for Belzebuth, so to speak, appears to relate to the 'three in one' mystery of the Trinitas.

The account of Nambroth in the *Wellcome MS* is interesting in this respect. It is in this text, as mentioned, that Belzebuth, complete with *Verum* conjuration, appears immediately before the account of the week. The account of Monday gives the *Verum* form of Lucifer's conjuration before that from *Honorius*, and goes so far as to recommend the former. The account of Astaroth on Wednesday differs, in among other things the absence of the *Verum* conjuration. In *Verum* meanwhile Belzebuth is attributed to Tuesday, preceded by Lucifer on Monday and followed by Astaroth on Wednesday.

These are our three chiefs who represent aspects of the mystery of the Trinitas. It is thus truly worthy of remark that Nambroth is described in the *Wellcome MS* as a fourth ruler, subordinate to the three others, and with the rank of Baron. This particular rank is interesting enough, since it does not otherwise appear in the feudal rankings associated with grimoire spirits from one text to another. Other interesting and enlightening details concerning Nambroth are found in this same text. He is associated with Tuesday under a New Moon in regal Leo; his character is made on a thin lead plate. There are characters on this plate, including those of the Moon, Leo, and Saturn, the planet ruling lead. However, the commentary on the spirit mentions him appearing on **Saturday** with the Moon in Leo 'as you may see in his character'. This apparent slip may be no such thing, and should be born in mind for later aspects of the discussion. The connection of a Baron with Saturday will have alerted those with an interest in Haitian traditions already.

That Frimost is an important figure in the *Verum* pantheon has been established previously (see *TG* and *TCM*), but an outline of his role is necessary here. Of primary importance is the employment of his sigil on the elder wand, that of evocation, identical with the 'staff' as present in other versions of the *Key of Solomon*. This bestows quite extraordinary significance on Frimost, parallel to the account of Baron Nambroth, in relation to the three chiefs. The *Wellcome MS 4666*'s variation on the Three Chiefs, complimented by a fourth, is an important variant, comparable to the Four Chiefs of the *Hygromanteia*. This clearly reflects themes in both GV and GH hierarchies, but is also a useful handle on a far wider context.

WELLCOME MS COMPARED WITH HYGROMANTEIA

Chief	Rank	Part of the World	Hygromantic Precedent
Lucifer	Emperor	Europe	Lucifer rules the East (thus over Oriens, who in turn is above Bael in later catalogues)
Belzebuth	Prince	Asia	Belzeboul rules the South (thus over Amaymon)
Astaroth	Count	Americas	Astaroth rules the West (thus over Paimon)
Nambroth	Baron	Libya (ancient N. Africa) and Mount Etna*	Asmodeus** rules the North (thus over Egyn)

* The relevance of this attribution to certain themes in *Geosophia* is significant.
** Apparently reduced to a king under Amaymon in later texts, his higher status is explored in TCM. It should be understood that the sources are not entirely resolvable into an Ur text, and the variations are better embraced as signposts of a Mystery; rather than reduced to a 'clear' but lifeless system. This is the way of mythology, and demonology is no exception.

The high status of Frimost aka Nambroth is underlined by other features of his background. These are examined by Owen Davies, after discussing the popularity of the Clavicule (*Verum*) and *Honorius* among Parisian mages.

> An obscure text that also cropped up several times in police investigations was dedicated to a spirit named Membrock or Manbrok.
>
> Owen Davies, *Grimoires: A History of Magic Books* p96-7

He gives an account of a renegade monk who in 1700 baptised his grimoire in the name of Manbrok. The details of the operation are also interesting, involving a chalk circle and a Mass said at the site on three consecutive days. A contemporary Parisian sorcerer was similarly engaged in conjuring Membrok at this time. On page 100 Davies identifies this Membrok aka Manbrok with the Nambrot of the C18th French *Honorius*. There are of course Solomonic links in MSS predating the first known printed *Verum*, as noted by both Rankine and Peterson. There Frimost appears as Frimoth in *Lansdowne 1202* and Frimolh (sic?) in *Wellcome MS 4669*. In my opinion at least some of these materials are adapted from a proto-*Verum*. This is supported by the fact that the highly composite *Wellcome 4666's* conjurations of the chiefs are identical to the printed edition, despite displacing Belzebuth through imitating *Honorius*. That *Verum* is in many respects a more coherent system than the MSS is also noteworthy.

The baptism of a grimoire in the name of a spirit is extremely significant. Several books of the *Bibliotheque bleue* are distinguished by an authorisation from one of the higher ranking spirits. Davies mentions and illustrates other examples with a handwritten pact on the title page. So too the baptism of grimoires in the lake of the Sybil in Norcia bears comparison (see *Geosophia*). Thus it is another mark of the status of Frimost that his namesakes shared this honour with Astaroth, Agliarept, and Lucifuge Rofocale. Strangely enough I was unaware of this precedent before publication of my *True Grimoire*, which bears Frimost's imprimatur for reasons of my own.

WEDNESDAY – ASTAROTH

The third day, Wednesday, is consistently attributed to Astaroth throughout the variants. Interestingly the German *Honorius* concurs with the opinion that Astaroth – among other spirits – is female. Astaroth is the third of the chiefs as known from *Verum* and other 'goetic' grimoires. In *Verum* she, Lucifer, and Belzebuth each possess unique conjurations, derived from the cryptography of Abbot Trithemius. Astaroth, and her conjuration, form a significant part of the lore surrounding the spirits of the seven days. These, as is apparent already, have some relation to the superior spirits of various grimoire hierarchies, that of the *True Grimoire* not least of them. Her deputies are Sargatanas and Nebirots; Sargatanas ruling Frucissiere, Guland, and Surgat, while Nebiros rules Morail, Frutimiere, and Huictigaras. In the *Grand Grimoire* Sargatanas rules Morax, Valefor, and Zoray, while Nebirots rules Ayperos, Cerberus, and Glasyabolas. Nebirots and the three spirits last named also appear in a spell together, probably modelled on the patterns found in the *Verum* tradition.

Astaroth is the third of the great chiefs, and by far the most readily contacted and worked with. This does not diminish the care and respect necessary in magical operations under her auspices.

One aspect of the invocation of the Trinitas that requires underlining is that in Cyprian grimoires and elsewhere the three chiefs are frequently invoked together in various forms of spellwork. This fact is a key to understanding the spirits of the seven days. Spells involving Frimost, Bechaud, Nebiros, Guland, and Surgat are also readily found in the various texts associated with these spirits, as demonstrated in my *True Grimoire*. This leaves Silcharde as the only spirit named for whom a role in spellwork is not already known from available sources.

THURSDAY – SIRCHADE AKA SILCHARDE

Thursday is variously attributed to Acham or to Silcharde. It is more or less reasonable to assume these spirits are identical. As mentioned above, so far no spells have come to light employing Silcharde, who is exceptional in this respect. However, as shown in *TG*, his sigil appears at the top of the pact used in the trial of Urban Grandier. In *Verum* style conjurations the pact is composed with the sigil of Scirlin at the top, and all spellwork relies on pacts. Further, there appears to be a link between Scirlin and another major spirit named in *Verum*, namely Duke Syrach. As will be shown shortly, a variant of Silcharde's name is Syrachael – Syrach with the typical angelic 'el' attached. The intermediary role of Scirlin requires comparison with the identical role for Oriens in *Livre de Esprits*. This identifies him as a chief of spirits, and strengthens the association with Syrach. Furthermore, with a Monday start point, Thursday is centre of the week; dividing the three chiefs from the spirits of the remaining days. Thus a unique and central role for Sirchade, understood to represent Scirlin/Syrach, is a workable interpretation.

FRIDAY – BECHET

Friday, like Wednesday, is consistent throughout the variants. Bechet, give or take spelling differences, appears here in each *Honorius* and in *Verum* alike. Like several other spirits of the days, Bechet is associated with one of the magical weapons: the sacrificial knife. The spirit is a subordinate of Agliarept, and invoked with Elelogap (Eliogaphatel) in spells for the making of rain (*Lansdowne 1202*).

> 12. To make Rain.
> [From the *Third Book of Solomon*]
>
> Take marinated [or marine; i.e. sea] water, natural or artificial, and put it in a circle which you will make on the earth, in the manner which is marked in the chapter on circles, in the middle of your circle put your Heliotrope stone, and on the right put your wand marked as described above, write the sigils of Bechard on the left side, and of Eliogaphatel [Elelogap] in the middle, and holding the wand you pronounce: "Eliogaphatel above heaven [or Eliogaphatel that is in heaven] give the clouds wings that they may resolve [in the old sense, 'separate, thaw, loosen'] in water". When these words are pronounced rain will fall in abundance. The marinated water can also be made by taking river water and adding a little salt with a little mud, and boil it for 15 minutes on the fire whilst throwing in a little pumice stone.

That 'Bechet' is a high status spirit is a fair assumption, a King or President most likely, and one of the Spirit Council. Rulership of a day, association with a major magical instrument and employment in a spell are all indications that we are dealing with an important spirit here. This makes it all the more surprising that identifying him or her elsewhere is exceedingly difficult. The very consistency of the day spirit accounts, in three forms of *Honorius* plus the Italian *Verum*, reduces the information. Friday is in any case the least detailed case. As if to signify this paucity, the sacrifice to Bechet is a nut.

One possible lead, to which I did not initially give much weight, is a similarly named spirit in the *Heptameron*. Burchat is an angel ruling in the West on Sunday. This possibility becomes less tenuous when we notice that the lists of angels concerned are frequently headed by recognisable planetary angels. In the case of Burchat, this is Anael, a Venusian angel (aka Haniel); appropriate to Friday, which Bechet rules. Nevertheless, there remains a great dearth of information, and it is my hope that more information comes to light. In the meantime, the most detailed account of Bechaud is undoubtedly *Verum*'s main spirit catalogue. The following is the synthesis form from my *True Grimoire*:

> Bechaud, also known as Bechet, Bechar or Bechard, has power over storms, tempests, rain, snow and hail, and other natural forces; over winds, frosts, thunderstorms, rains of blood, and of toads and other species. Also said: he controls all kinds of weather, be it wind, hail, rain or tempest, and will serve you with any weather, for any task. Honorius says of him that he requires a walnut in sacrifice.

SATURDAY – NEBIROS, GULAND

Saturday in this tradition is attributed in some texts to Nabam who appears to be another form of Nambroth, attributed to Tuesday. It is doubtful that this extends to outright identity, and obviously the rituals and timing are quite different. Nevertheless, the above mentioned indications in *Wellcome MS 4669* are highly interesting. Other texts call the spirit of Saturday Nebiros aka Nebirots, which is likely an alternative form of Nabam. Indeed, there are cryptic references to a second Nebirots in the GV, likely indicating the same Tuesday and Saturday polarity in vestigial form.

Another spirit associated with Saturday in these texts is Guland. Whether he is to be identified with the above or seen as separate is a moot point. As seen with other days, the schema is perhaps not as straightforward as appears. He is frequently paired with the spirit Surgat, for example their sigils are inscribed on the Liming Pot to be discussed anon. They also appear in malefic spells together. As will be seen in due course, Surgat is a particularly interesting spirit concerning whom there is a great deal to be said. For this reason we should not be too ready to jump to conclusions, and be ready for more surprises as investigation of the spirit catalogues accelerates.

Operations involving subordinates of Nebiros are readily performed on this day. An interesting and important conjuration including them appears in the Italian *Verum*. This is referenced later in the current work, and as will be noted it names eighteen spirits; this involves a recurring theme in various grimoires which has not been explained so far in modern works.

> Their Conjuration:

> Serguthy, Heramael, Trimasael, Sustugriel; Agalieraps, Tarithimal, Elgo-apa, Nebiros, Hael, and Sergulath; and you also Proculo, Haristum, Brulefer, Pentagnegni, Aglasis, Sidragosam, Minosums and Bucons, come together by the Great, Powerful and Holy Adonay, thou shalt appear, come, by the will and command of N... N... and bring all your power, place yourselves in the power of he who calls, heeding all that he desires.

> Sanctus, Sanctus Regnum Verba praeterague nihil! Omnis spiritus rexurgat! Pa voluntas, fiat voluntate mea.

> [Holy, Holy Royal Word, surpassed by none! All ye spirits arise, come peacefully and do my will.]

SUNDAY – SURGAT

Surgat, spirit of Sunday in *Honorius*, is one of a variety of names by which one of the major spirits of the catalogues is known. As the catalogues and their spirits have received insufficient critical attention to date, a full discussion requires other matters to be introduced.

REGARDING THE FOUR KINGS

BEFORE RESUMING some of the introduced themes, attention is directed back to the structure of the implicit hierarchy in back of several well known and not so well known grimoires. This 'standard' (which actually includes numerous variations, some yet to be drawn out) begins with three chiefs. Following them are four Kings, a term which, confusingly, is also applied to another level of the hierarchy to follow. These would require a very major discussion in themselves. Until recently this would have been necessary in order to make many would be 'goetians' aware of their role in tradition in the first place. At present this task is already accomplished in large part in *TCM*. It would take us too far from our theme to cover them again in the depth required; much of the former work must therefore be taken as a given.

In short, they reprise in the grimoires themes established in Late Antiquity, involving both Egyptian and Syrian ideas about the stations of the Sun, and the Four Winds. In mythological guises these comprise four distinct persons with an implicit fifth 'pantheistic' figure above them. This latter figure may be traced in the character of Satan in the current schema; anciently, in purely solar guise (rather than the sublunar form) a more appropriate figure would be Helios-Apollo, or Sol-Invictus. The grimoires however reflect the earlier, indeed prehistoric, forms of goetia where the so called 'sub lunar' sphere – unadulterated by 'transcendental' ideas, was the principal matter of interest.

This goes a long way also to explain why some forms of the trinity are LBS and others LBA, since Astaroth – reprising aspects of Hecate and perhaps Lilith – is the female form of the superior fifth figure, the ultimate ruler of ghosts and spirits of the same sub lunar, or aerial, sphere. Traces of 'Lunar pantheism' co-existing in antiquity with 'solar-pantheism' – for example in the PGM – centre on Hecate. I suspect the book burnings at Ephesus are more to be regretted than the loss of Alexandria's library in this respect, among others.

Some brief notes are however required for our Four Kings here in skeletonic 'inter-catalogue' form. A more extended discussion of a major under-examined variant of one of them then follows.

ORIENS, PAYMON, AMAYMON, EGYN

Livre des Esperitz	Book of Offices	Others
Orient	Orience/Oriens	Found in Agrippa, *Abramelin*, *clm 849*, *ms. Plut.89 Sup.38*, *ToS* (recension C) and others.

Oriens is the great ruler of the East par excellence, variants notwithstanding. *Honorius* has Magoa or Nagoa (sic), likely a variant of Magot, an old high status spirit from early catalogues. All the variant names likely need tracking down – not simply taken as a) wrong or b) automatically aliases. A link with the solar pantheism of Late Antiquity, linked to the four directions, is virtually certain.

Livre des Esperitz	Book of Offices	Others
Poymon	Paymon	As above. Bayemon, Bayemont. *Honorius*

Paimon, variously spelled, is the most usual great ruler of the West, again, variants notwithstanding. David Rankine points out that the unusual spelling in *Honorius* has the same pronunciation in French as Paymon (*CGH*).

Livre des Esperitz	Book of Offices	Others
Amoymon	Amaymon	As above

Maymon, the King and 'angel' of Saturn's day in the *Heptameron*, is a likely counterpart for this King; linkage of the *Heptameron* with Arabic grimoires where days also have an angel and demon attributed are very clear here: Kasfiael for Cassiel and Mimoun for Maymon. Attempts to associate Amaymon with the New Testament's 'Mammon' fade to nothing compared to such textual evidences. Note that his southern rulership connects him with Capricorn, which is ruled by Saturn. *Honorius* atypically attributes Amaymon to the North and Egym to the South.

Livre des Esperitz	Book of Offices	Others
Equi	Egin	Found in Agrippa, *clm 849*, *ms. Plut.89 Sup.38*, *ToS* (recension C) and others

Abramelin has Ariton, see essay following. It may be unwise to assume this spirit is simply an alter ego of Egyn without further data.

ARITON

When in the rosy morn Arcturus shines
Then pluck the clusters from the parent vines.

Hesiod, *Works and Days*.

A DISTRACTION from my work on *The Testament of Cyprian the Mage* had unexpected results relevant to its themes. Research into Traditional Witchcraft and lore involving characters linked to Azazel, and thus to the Four Kings, led me to an examination of the circumpolar constellations. In particular, my researches involved the constellation Boötes. This constellation contains the major Fixed Star, Arcturus, one of the "Fifteen Behenian Stars" with sigil and correspondences mentioned at various points in other volumes.

So, I followed up. Boötes, (or its principal star, it is often hard to tell which), has a classical title, namely Arator. This is phonetically similar to Ariton, one of two names associated with the King of the North, and to Aratron, the Olympic Spirit of Saturn. Circumpolar stars were considered important in both Egyptian and Mesopotamian lore, a status perpetuated at least in part in the papyri and Hermetica.

Arcturus was one of the first stars to be named and appears from the earliest times in astronomical writings. In Babylonian myth the star was associated with a form of the god Enlil, whose wife Ninlil similarly was associated with Ursa Major. Enlil was strongly associated with farming, appropriate to Aratron, whose 'pagan' counterpart, the god Saturn, was also strongly connected to agriculture. Enlil was a kingly god, and associated with the moist spring wind that softened the earth for the hoe or plough, both instruments being connected to him (Ursa Major is the 'Plough'; Enlil invented the hoe or mattock). A King of moistening winds is at very least appropriate to a King of spirits linked to winds (as all four are) and to moisture (North, where Ariton is attributed, is associated with water in the traditional correspondences). Arcturus is also associated with storms, presumably watery ones, and is said to be unfortunate for sea voyages, likely for the same reason.

In both Greek and Mesopotamian myth, the constellation Boötes is male and Ursa Major female; the two are also linked in familial relations. An astrologer correspondent of mine with a background in Babylonian lore made the further remark that the Sumerian plough was typically hung from the roof of the barn – resembling the high position of the Plough constellation in the 'Northern Height' of the sky.

It appears highly likely that Ariton is linked to both Aratron and the title of Arcturus, Arator. Whether or not Egyn aka Egin, another more frequently encountered name for the Northern king, is identical with Ariton is as yet unknown. Egyn possesses at least two sigils, one from *Clavis Inferni* and another from the Biblioteca Medica Laurenziana's *ms. Plut.89 Sup.38*. Connecting Ariton, who previously had no sigil, with Aratron and Arator (Arcturus) provides two sigils for him also. Agrippa says that the star is of the nature of Mars 'when the Sun's aspect is full towards it', and Jupiter 'when the contrary'. Images of a wolf or horse, both creatures of Mars, are made under this star which 'is good against fevers, and astringeth and retaineth the blood'. Mars of course is associated with the nocturnal sect (as is the Northern sign Cancer) and with elemental water. Ebertin gives Arcturus a dual Jupiter-Mars classification. He credits it with obtaining 'Justice through power', making the native belligerent and quarrelsome, particularly if conjunct one or other of these planets. An outgoing and competitive character is indicated. Bad aspects can induce losses through litigation. The benign Fixed Star, Spica, has a very similar longitude, but a great difference in latitude. Working with Spica – the most benign of all Fixed Stars – can benefit from Arcturean influence, which also represents hard work, as appropriate to the image of a ploughman or farmer.

THE SPIRIT COUNCIL

THE BOOK OF OFFICES appears in *The Book of Oberon*, and was influential on various English mss including Rudd's; it was also transcribed separately by Frederick Hockley, influential at a later time. My research began with Hockley's transcription, edited by Colin Campbell. This edition has the advantage of including an important table absent from *Oberon* (p64 Appendix One). Some differences in spelling or transcription between this version and *Oberon* do not complicate things overmuch. Incidentally, I have compared my findings following Hockley with JHP's identifications of spirits in *The Book of Oberon*, and wherever we have both considered particular spirits our independent identifications concur without exception.

The Book of Offices is evidently a closely related form of the book from which Weyer obtained his materials, save that in many respects its hierarchy is more complete and untampered, enabling a more meticulous reconstruction and many clarifications. Predating Weyer, the presence of such a book in England as well as the Continent, before the *Goetia* was produced, is certain. The material as we have it essentially consists of two catalogues. Both provide a great deal of information, although the second is more structurally important. Additional information concerning ranks, and more importantly the roles they indicate can be mined from both catalogues.

In list one, the names appear to be organised more or less in order of rank. This is useful for various reasons. In the second listing the spirits are arranged according to King and Direction, a tremendous improvement on the *Goetia* and even *The Book of Spirits*. Preceding all there is an account of the three chiefs; then the Four Kings are described, along with their kings, counsellors, and messengers. This is where the clarity is balanced by more confusion. Some, but not all of these 'messengers', can be identified in the tables. The matter is further confused in the incantations, where presidents, kings or messengers are jumbled and shared quite frequently. The table in Appendix One from *Sloane MS 3824*, rightly or no, describes the kings as messengers (compare 'guides', see Long Texts p. 133 and Gaap entry). Close equivalents to this table can be found in *KGM* which plainly draws on this text or a close relative. I combine various such lists below to facilitate reference with important identifications to follow. The so called 'method of Hochma' as it stands, is, I believe, an English attempt to reconstruct an earlier hierarchical process of conjuration, something inadequately detailed in the continental texts that survive. As such it deserves our close attention, even if with a fair degree of caution.

Caution because, on the face of it, a group of spirits has appeared as an additional layer of 'messengers'. None are familiar from the catalogues as such; I refer to Temel, Emelon, Ocar, Cydaton, Madycon, Rombalane, Rodabelles and their variants. These may represent an unknown part of the operating process native to our catalogues; then again, they may not. Some are possibly aliases; however, the likelihood is they are simply superfluous additions. This suspicion is shown amply by *Sloane MS 3824*; while in Weyer and the *Goetia*, Paimon is attended by two kings, in MS 3824 we are told to expect five.

However, the spirits involved in this 'infernal multiplication' are not without interest. Temel may well be Tamiel from *The Book of Enoch*, whose name was also transliterated thus in Schodde's translation; Tamiel teaches astrology. Rodabelles resembles 'spiritus iocundissimus' Rodobail/Rodobayl from *clm 849* no.6 (for obtaining a banquet). In the note to *Offices* 2, Bealphares may be in the process of being added to the schema; to appear in the Council as Belfarto (and almost immediately getting duplicated as Belferth). Nevertheless, again, Belferith is conjured in *clm 849*. No.2 (for causing a person to lose his senses). There is also a possibility that Belferith is actually Belberith (Berith), and already represented – in both catalogues and council – before being added again. Though some are recognisable spirits, at present, by and large the role of these 'messengers' appears to be an extra intermediary stage in the conjuration process. That is, the role of these messengers is apparently to talk to other messengers. This level of redundancy has no apparent parallel in the earlier catalogues and grimoires.

At some point an editor – probably the same one – appears to have experimented with reducing this new flock of messengers to one. This is Mirage, whose name is spelled slightly differently depending on which king he is working for (Marage, Merage and so on). Here too there is confusion in the text, apparently with not enough alternative spellings listed to go around. Nonetheless, Mirage is known, from *clm 849* No.32, where the name is apparently a synonym of Satan. Against this, Satan of course is already present in this system, and holds a significantly higher rank.

Thus, for the most part, I am happy at present to leave this particular aspect of the English paper trail alone. My interest resides in other approaches to the hierarchical system in conjuring methodology.

This brings us to the concept of the 'Presidential Council' itself; a structure with two components, the Council, and the Messengers. The concept originates or is closely linked with *Offices*, so is of course prior to Rudd. Although the above mentioned spirits are involved with the second part of this structure, it plainly derives from consideration of the catalogues and an effort to reconstruct the hierarchical layers needed for conjuration. Having agonised over the obscurities in Weyer, let alone the *Goetia*, I can empathise with this effort, and aspects of the approach are legitimate by my lights. In short, it makes sense in terms of the timing *Observations* in Weyer/Scot, with hierarchical and vital intermediary principles in ritual, among other indicators.

Even given my reservations about the second part, where there is possible – or likely – elaboration, the idea of a Presidential Council should not be disregarded on that account. It includes some important pointers which likely relate to earlier phases of development. The essentials of this material are something like this:

There are Four Kings: Oriens, Paymon, Amaymon and Egin.

Their Presidential Councillors are: Niopheyn, Barbas, Sebarbas, Alilgon, Gordonizer, Tame, Vassago, Othey, Um, Anaboth, Aleche, Berith, Mala.

Whose messengers are: Baal, Temel, Belfarto or Belferit, Balferth [likely duplicating the previous name], Belial, Bawson, Rombulence or Ramblane, Alphasis, Boulon, Ocarbidaton, Madicon.

In identifying these spirits allowance must be made for both differences of spelling and variant names. Then the 'Presidential Council' consists entirely of names occurring in our catalogues. Only the 'messengers' section appears to have been, as I presently consider it, overly reconstructed. A certain caution with the Council is needed as – for example – presently there is no evidence Vassago was part of the Continental tradition, but the essentials of this part of the table are both important and fascinating. As for the second section, plainly the catalogues themselves intended the various kings such as Baal, Curson – only some of whom are included here – in the role of so called 'messengers'. 'Messengers' indicates intermediary spirits, those with authority over the followers of a superior; as Baal for Oriens, and so on.

Thus our best course for this second part of the equation is to unravel the mysteries surrounding these Kings, who were and are an integral part of the system from inception. Meanwhile the first part, the actual 'councillors', obviously relates to such things as the rank and timing *Observations* of the operating process. It is also extremely useful in fine tuning some of the identifications of the spirits.

Some variants of this Council are worth mentioning. The *Grimoire of Arthur Gauntlet* contains what appears to be an important variant of the 'Presidential Council'. It contains approximately the same number of similar names: Sulphur, Chalcos, *Anaboth, Sonenel, Barbaros, Gorson/ Gorzon*, Everges, *Mureril, Vassago, Agares*, Baramper and *Barbazan*.

Several of these spirit names cast light on the *Offices/Oberon* catalogue. Thus Gorson/Gorzon identifies Gordonizer/Gordosar, an otherwise mysterious figure from the *Offices* form of the Presidential Council. Meanwhile Sonenel is very likely Synoryell, and Mureril is Muryell. This is very useful data, casting considerable light on the Council and the difficulties and gaps involved with the Northern part of the hierarchy (in *Offices/Oberon* and far beyond). So too, *Sloane 3824*'s version of the Conjuration of Bealpharos/Bealphares mentions an Alpherez (Alphasis?) and Baramper (see *BTS*).

Meanwhile the 'tables' appearing in the sources mentioned are scant on detail and inter-relations between Kings and Presidents. I provide on page 56 a more useful tabulation, not merely of names, but their aliases, ranks, and known directions. Note that if Vassago's rank is read as Prince=President it appears that spirits of three specific ranks are involved. See later section on Ranks of the Spirits (p. 69).

Note that in the Cyprianic version of the *Grand Grimoire* three intermediary spirits below the six deputies are named: Mirion, Belial, and Anagaton. Of these we can readily identify Belial, who is of course a King (and thus a Messenger). Mirion may be equivalent to Mirage, and Anagaton possibly to Ocarbidaton, for whom see page 53.. These two are not readily identified elsewhere in the catalogues, but the reference is worth citing (see my TCM for details).

Similarly, in the *Heptameron* or *Magical Elements of Saint Cyprian*, also examined in TCM, we find Baalberith given as a chief spirit in dream experiences, complete with subordinates. As already noted, Baalberith may be a form of Berith, already worthy of consideration for addition to the list of Kings (aka Messengers). From these considerations it appears likely enough that the spirit Belferit referenced here (and the multiple confused aliases) should be identified with Baalberith.

Councillor	Weyer/*Goetia* form	Rank	Direction *Offices* 2
Niopheyn aka Neophon	Glasyabolas	President	East
Barbas/Marbas/Corbas	Barbas	President	East
Sebarbas/Barbatos/Barbais	Barbatos	Duke	East
Alilgon/Algor	Eligor	Duke	East
Gordonizer/Gordoser	Curson	King	West
Tame/Layme/Zayme	Raum, Raim *	President	West
Vassago/Usagoo	Vassago	Prince (according to Offices) and Marquis	North**
Othey			North
Um			North
Anaboth	Furcas ***	President	North
Aleche/Abech/Elyeth/Ebeyeth		King	South
Berith	Berith	Duke	South
Mala/Mallapar	Malphas	President	South

* Note that Caim (Pres) and Raim (Earl) are consecutive entries in Weyer. They have a not dissimilar appearance and the same number of legions; probably conflation or other complicating factors are at work. See main entries.

** See *Book of Treasure Spirits* (Sloane MS 3825): Vassago swears by his king 'Baro the king of the West'. A Western attribution renders this table much more symmetrical. Attributing Vassago to the West leaves identifiable Northern spirits thin on the ground; finding Falcas aka Surgat aka Azael there more than makes up for it.

*** The dual nature of this spirit deserves thorough investigation, see main entry.

THE
SPIRIT CATALOGUES
PART ONE

LBA AND 'EIGHTEEN-NESS'

IN THE CURRENT 'grimoire revival' a great deal of attention has been paid to authors, real and mythical, to manuscripts and fine books, to collecting impedimenta. Significantly less academic attention has been paid to the spirits, many of whom appear right across the genre thus analysed, and their part in our tradition and its history. My primary intention here is to discuss the connections between spirit catalogues in several grimoires, the relations between spirits as well as their ranks and functions within the system. Given that this involves multiple fragments and variants on a 'theme', with underlying patterns to be rediscovered, it would be very easy to get bogged down in detail. Cross references will undoubtedly be a part of any elucidation, but ideally a place to start and expand from is required. For various reasons, this place is with the so called 'blue' grimoires, the *Grimorium Verum* and the *Grand Grimoire*. These, with the equally notorious *Grimoire of Pope Honorius*, represent a 'family' of grimoires; for reasons to be elucidated shortly, this group shall be termed LBA.

Various writers, whose works are at the forefront of grimoire studies, have touched on the matter of Chiefs over the spirits. To recap, there is a fairly stable grouping of principal spirits. It is found, with variants, in groups of either three or four. This implicit upper hierarchy is incredibly persistent in a large family of grimoires in several languages, beginning with Greek, Latin, a variety of European languages, and early English manuscripts.

From here the texts either take or imply two principal forms, whose close relations I mean to clarify. In some forms, subordinate to these Chiefs, not necessarily on a one to one basis, are also found Four Kings. This is not always clearly delineated; indeed one major source text apparently scrambled the details deliberately (Weyer) as well as making omissions. Nevertheless, texts such as the French *Le Livre des Esperitz*, or the earlier English catalogue in *The Book of Offices*, reveal a clearer picture of the system underlying the *Goetia of Solomon*. In this form, there are three chiefs: Lucifer, Belzebuth, and Satan (LBS); also Four Kings: Oriens, Amaymon, Paymon, and Egin.

Another form, not at first glance related, also begins with three Chiefs: Lucifer, Belzebuth, and Astaroth (LBA). It gives each of them two deputies, and then gives a shorter catalogue of subordinate spirits. Two important examples of this format are the *Grand Grimoire* and its variants, and the equally influential *Grimorium Verum*. Two earlier Solomonic MSS with strong structural resemblances to both have nowadays been published (*Lansdowne 1202* and *Wellcome 4669*). Mathers believed the *Grimorium Verum* to have influenced these, rather than vice versa. More recently some have assumed they are the source of the grimoire; in my opinion this is an error caused by comparative neglect of the spirit catalogues, or 'dramatis personæ'. In other words, Mathers had a point.

There are problematic aspects to the resemblance of these MSS to the grimoires mentioned that remain to be explained. *Verum* for example gives at points a far clearer account of the 'shared' catalogue than either of the MSS, and likely derives from a more complete, currently unknown text. The MSS are not simply at an earlier stage of development as might be assumed. Close examination shows actual omissions in the spirit listings, particularly in its latter parts. The omission in both MSS of eight spirits under Hacel and Sergulas might be explained by being an earlier stage. However, both MSS also provide sigils for four spirits under Satanachi while omitting their powers, an error of transmission not present in the grimoire. With two of these four spirits now identified, and the material proven correct, the GV clearly had another more complete source than is currently known.

Turn now from the differences to the similarities. The closest resemblance between the two MSS and our grimoires is in the account each gives of the upper part of the hierarchy. Here three chiefs are set over up to six deputies. Note that the Astaroth of the grimoires is called Elestor in these MSS; a detail well worth bearing in mind. Other names however are mostly similar to identical. The comparison is revelatory.

DEPUTIES OF THE CHIEFS

Chiefs / Texts	Lucifer		Belzebuth		Astaroth (Elestor in the MSS)	
Wellcome 4669	Sirachi	Satanachia	Agaterop	Hymateh	Stephanuta	Resbiroth
Lansdowne 1202	Sirachi	Satanachi	Agateraptor	Himacth (and Stephanuta)		
Grimorium Verum	Satanachia	Agliarept	Tarchimache	Fleurity	Sargatanas	Nesbirots
Grand Grimoire	Lucifuge Rofocale	Satanachia	Agliarept	Fleurety	Sargatanas	Nebiros

As can be seen, this table clarifies the identity of Duke Syrach named in the *Grimorium Verum*. It also makes him directly equivalent to Lucifuge Rofocale in the *Grand Grimoire*. As regards the allocation of deputies, the latter grimoire, bar the Duke's change of name, is closer to both of the MSS. It is worth noting that as traditionally described, Leonard, the Prince of the Sabbat, is identical in appearance with Lucifuge Rofocale. In the Iberian grimoire, *The Magical Elements of Saint Cyprian* (see TCM) he appears in much the same role as his counterpart in the above grimoires. It is necessary to elucidate this point, as it is of some importance in relation to other factors to emerge later. In my *Testament of Cyprian the Mage* the following appears:

> Leonard, although sporting a name that scarcely suggests diabolism, is identical with the Sabbat goat worshipped by the witches. Under this name he is reckoned by various demonologists as: the chief of the minor demons (those attending sabbats presumably) and the Inspector General of Black Magic and Sorcery. He is said to have had three horns and the ears of a fox. Witches saluted him by exposing their buttocks while holding in their hands a green candle.

Two plates from the *Grand Grimoire* and *Red Dragon* cycle illustrate a treasure bearing demon with three horns; one of these portraits has the signature of Lucifuge Rofocale beneath. This identifies Leonard and Lucifuge; conflating - with good reason - the lore of the Sabbat with the sorcery of the late grimoires. The inquisitorial accusation that witches made pacts precedes the plain rendition of the process in the later grimoires (a rendition preceded by the more covert 'Book of Spirits', which as seen is a comprehensive pact). Indeed, as has been established, the concept of the pact reaches back to the magicians of antiquity; be they the sorcerers of the *PGM* seeking a 'magical assistant', or the theurgists with their covenants. While a staple of theological opposition to magic, the conception originates in magic of the synthesis period if not before.

Thus, to resume, as Duke Syrach, Sirachi is mentioned in the *Grimorium Verum*. Also, a list of eighteen spirits is given, over which he is said to rule. A similar list of spirits appears in the two MSS mentioned above. Simplifying this material, we can readily compare them in a table, as follows, using the order of spirits given in the French editions of *Verum*, as the Italian order is somewhat different and less reliable.

LÉONARD, FROM JACQUES COLLIN DE PLANCY'S *DICTIONNAIRE INFERNAL*

Spirits of Syrach – *Grimorium Verum*

GV (French)	Lansdowne 1202 KoS	Wellcome MS 4669 KoS	Aliases elsewhere
Claunech	Elantiel, Chaunta	Elanthil, Chaunta	
Musisin	Resochin, Roschim	Rosochim, Roschim	
Bechaud	Bechar	Beschard	Bechet GH. Very possibly Burchat *Heptameron*.
Frimost	Frimoth	Frimolh	Frimost, Nambroth GH
Klepoth	Klepoth, Kepoth		
Khil	Klic, Kleim		
Mersilde	Mertiel, Inertiel	Mertiel	
Clisthert	Sirumel, Selytarel	Syrumel, Slittareth	
Sirchade	Sirechael	Syrechael*	Silchade GH
Hiepact	Hepoth	Stepoth	
Humots	Humet	Stumet	
Segal	Fegot	Fegol	
Frucissiere	Frulhel, Frastiel	Frastiel	
Guland	Galant	Galoneti	Guland GH
Surgat	Surgatha	Surgatha	Surgat GH, Parcas GoS and many others
Morail	Menail	Menail	Possibly Merail (Saturday spirit, *Hygromanteia*)
Frutimier	Glitia	Glitia	
Huictigaras	——		

* Note resemblance of this name to Syrach.

As can be seen, the French grimoire's list is more complete than both the MSS. Both MSS omit Huictigaras, and one omits Klepoth and Khil. As mentioned, other omissions in a subsequent spirit list suggest incomplete copying rather than an earlier stage in development. Also notice that when the demonstrably earlier *Grimoire of Honorius* involves spirits from this list, it prefers the *Verum* spellings. These indications and others suggest that the *Verum* hierarchy precedes the MSS rather than vice versa and may be considered an important source in its own right.

To recap, before using this basis to move onwards, in this system there are chiefs, a chief has two deputies, and the deputies have 'subordinate' spirits. These so called subordinates are often accorded high ranks elsewhere, but we may leave that for now. The eighteen spirits detailed above have so far in the great majority of cases, *not* been identified with spirits from Weyer's catalogue and its relatives. The major exception is the spirit Surgat, who, as will be shown, has proven important right across the grimoire spectrum under various aliases. The important thing about this particular grimoire cycle (the *True* and the *Grand* grimoires), is that it not only names the spirits of various ranks, but details the relations between them and its role in the ritual process. This is done more explicitly and clearly than in any of the other grimoires we are to consider. Therefore, despite apparent differences, they provide an extremely useful point of departure when comparing and investigating across the wider genre.

KHIL, FRENCH VERUM

Eighteen-ness, the Grand Grimoire and Weyer

Note well that the 18 spirits discussed above are not directly equivalent to the first 18 of Weyer's spirits but to a different grouping entirely; the *Grand Grimoire* is another matter. This grimoire has the same three chiefs and a very similar set of deputies to the above. Its eighteen 'subordinate spirits' however are not those of the *Grimorium Verum* and its relatives, known or hypothetical. The 'subordinate spirits' of the *Grand Grimoire* exactly duplicates the first 18 spirits from Weyer's list, which are also the first 18 of *Livre des Esperitz*. This includes Pruslas, the spirit appearing in Weyer but omitted by Scot and the *Goetia*. Note that in *The Book of Offices*, of the 12 spirits listed as under Oriens no less than ten are from this group, and none fall outside that column. As will be seen, this does not exhaust the distribution or stability of this important group of spirits; with some variation this group appears persistently in a variety of texts and languages. This makes information regarding Eastern spirits the most consistent we have. It also virtually identifies Oriens with Syrach and Lucifuge Rofocale, with all that this identification would entail.

The Spirits

First 18 spirits from Weyer. (1).

compared with *Grand Grimoire*

Weyer's spirits with aliases	Rank given	*Grand Grimoire* (no ranks)
Bael	King	Bael
Agares	Duke	Agares
Marbas, Barbas	President	Marbas
Pruslas, Busas	Prince and duke	Pruslas
Amon, Aamon	Marquis	Amon
Barbatos	Count or earl and duke	Barbatos
Buer	President	Buer
Gusoyn	Duke	Gusoin
Botis, Otis	President and earl	Botis
Bathym (Bathin), Mathim	Duke	Bathin
Pursan (Purson) Curson	King	Purson
Eligor, Abigor	Duke	Eligos
Loray, Oray	Marquis	Loray
Valefar, Malephar	Duke	Valefar
Morax, Foraii	Earl, president	Foraii
Ipos, Ayperos	Earl, prince	Ipos
Naberus, (Naberius), Cerberus	Marquis	Naberius
Glassy- Labolas, Caacrinolas, Caasimolar	President	Glasya-labolas

Lucifuge Rofocale	Satanachia	Agliarept	Fleruty	Sargatanas	Nebiros
Bael	Pruslas	Buer	Bathin	Loray	Ipos
Agares	Amon	Gusoin	Purson	Valefar	Naberius
Marbas	Barbatos	Botis	Eligos	Foraii (Morax)	Glasya-Labolas

TIMING CONSIDERATIONS

AND THE RANKING SYSTEM

Trithemius speaks of a *Liber officiorum* that catalogues four
emperors and various kings, dukes, marquises and counts.

Forbidden Rites. Richard Kieckhefer

AS MENTIONED already, given times for conjuring various spirits are present
in major continental grimoires; they have a distinct nocturnal emphasis.
It is time now to analyse the quite distinct considerations given in Weyer,
Scot, and the *Goetia*. This is important for various reasons, as it casts
light on the relations existing between spirits and other subtleties. Even
if the timing system and ranks themselves are ultimately dispensable, the
ritual mechanisms they relate to are crucial.

The timing rules given in Weyer and Scot are slightly clearer and
also different from those in the *Goetia*. Indeed, it is my impression that
all English versions of the spirit hierarchy – such as *Off, KGM, Goetia* –
have reworked them with varying degrees of success. In order to bypass
some of the resulting confusion, these forms will mostly be left aside.
The system as delivered in the Weyer and Scot form is a surer guide to
original meaning and structure, one which grants new insights lost with
the old *Goetia*-centred approach.

The feudal ranks of the spirits, and their intended meaning, appear
to be closely related to these same original rules. The ranks of the spirits,
when closely examined, have a dual significance. They indicate when
the spirits may be called in the timing rules of particular grimoires. They
relate also to important ritual processes concerning intermediary spirits,
extending beyond the grimoires to which such timing rules apply. The
intermediary process involves major Kings being invoked before lesser
Kings and Presidents are conjured, frequently in order to deploy other
spirits appropriate to the time concerned. Texts such as *Oberon* and *KGM*
appear to have appreciated such a principle, although adding an extra
intermediary group of spirits (such as Temel and Emlon) unknown in
Weyer or related continental grimoires. A greater degree of complication
appears in these reconstructions, as well as confusion.

Of the system itself, it is to be noticed that the ranks relate to an almost entirely diurnal timing, not obviously appropriate to alleged demons. In fact, in several continental grimoires that employ nocturnal times for related or identical spirits, this system of ranking is not used. This highlights the intimacy between the use of the ranks and the timing rules given in Weyer and the English texts.

It is worth noting in passing that decans and spirit hierarchies have a long relationship. Nevertheless, the mostly diurnal timings firmly discounts interpreting fifty percent of the spirits as related to the decans 'by night' (as in Crowley's *Liber 777* and elsewhere). Similarly, attribution of the ranks to the planets (and vaguely appropriate metals) looks like a late ham-fisted addition and will be omitted here. Were a decan attribution to exist, or be devised, a far more even distribution of planets would be essential. As some of the ranks hardly exist this is not a great loss; indeed, it assists reappraisal of the spirits as separate from a particular book.

The following 'rules' cannot be considered as binding throughout the grimoires. Nevertheless, they are of considerable interest from numerous angles and both deserve and reward investigation.

In presenting these 'rules' here for practical use beside the tables, I have resisted the urge to substitute the names of the Four Kings Oriens/East, Paimon/West, Amaymon/South and Egyn/North. Nevertheless, texts in which these are specified as ruling the same spirits precede the much shortened and adulterated hierarchy of the *Goetia*. While some textual complications remain, for the most part taking these as given aids clarity. The subject is, frankly, complicated enough.

PRELATES

The timing rules for Prelates are retained, although, with one sole exception, appearing neither in Weyer nor the *Goetia* but in the *Book of Offices*, the rank does not occur. No prelates are mentioned in the entire Weyer catalogue; it is thus correspondingly absent from the *Goetia*. Taking its occurrence in the timing rules to represent another rank is a fix, not an answer. However, there is a solitary Prelate in the first listing in the *Book of Offices*, namely Boab or Boall. There is nothing particularly conspicuous to distinguish this spirit from the others; he rides a black horse so resembles a Duke. This may be where the trail ends, but there is another possibility.

Elsewhere in *Oberon* we find Boel or Boell, invoked as the angel of Saturday (pp232). Curiously enough these planetary conjurations are followed by correspondences and a list of pagan gods. Elsewhere in the text he is listed as one of the seven 'Senators' (pp278). This thread continues, the Senators appearing as invoked powers over demons (together with the Four Kings. pp302, 307, 311). Boel is a massively ancient spirit name of enormous status, appearing in the papyri. The ancient context overlaps considerably with the same solar pantheism involved with the Four Kings (and, indeed, Bael, see *TCM*) but appears as often in a sevenfold classification, the 'Chaldean' equivalents of the weekday gods we inherit from Late Antiquity.

This Boel appears in the angelic workings in *Oberon* which resemble the forms of the *Heptameron*, and mentions similar angels (for example, Uriel). While *Oberon* mentions the distinctly ambivalent 'angels of the day' (Maymon for Saturday for example) they do not appear in the conjurations. It is worth considering whether the Senators have taken their place. Certainly early forms of the *Goetia* overlap considerably with the *Heptameron*, and a group of seven semi-angelic demon Prelates is an interesting possibility.

KNIGHTS

The question of knights is also problematic. Firstly, there is no trace of them in *Livre des Esperitz*, and the one instance in Scot and the *Goetia* is probably erroneous, as will subsequently be shown. This is not the end of the matter, as there are a handful of knights in the first listing of the *Book of Offices*.

The most likely explanation for the rank's presence probably has nothing to do with planetary attributions or metals. This attribution apparently postdates the ranks themselves, and has little evident basis in the spirits abilities. What should probably be considered is the important grimoire 'subgenre' of separate processes; for example, the 'armigerous spirits' and their squires in the seventh experiment of *clm 849*. Similarly, *the experiment of the three knyghtes* (CBM) its barbarous names have some correspondence with incantations of the *Heptameron* and *Goetia*.

Such semi-folklorish processes are of course absent from Weyer and the *Goetia*, although a more extended forerunner could easily have included them. Spirits appearing in the catalogues are by no means unusual figures in just such folklorish processes. Scot's appendices are only one source of examples. Such 'experiments' are also a major part of *Oberon*, and common in the mss. The magical treasure hunting approach has close affinities with this genre, although all manner of purposes arise. In short, the timing rules could have been intended to accommodate such 'minor processes'. The spirits invoked may have held a variety of ranks (examples abound of experiments concerning kings and others). Thus we are essentially dealing with spirits who look like armed men, in trios, bands or singly, invoked in less formulaic and more 'mythical' or folklorish rituals.

This hypothesis has more to commend it than an uneven and dubious astrological overlay with no proven previous relation. On the other hand, while 'knights' may have had just such a previous role, it is essentially redundant in its current context. It is as well though to reappraise the entire feudal structure, before finally consigning any part of it to overdue oblivion. Discussion of the diverse ranks and their variants will be found elsewhere in this treatise.

THE TIMING RULES

Taking our text from Scot, the rules are given as follows:

> AMAYMON king of the east, Gorson king of the south, Zimimar king of the north, Goap king and prince of the west, may be bound from the third houre, till noone, and from the ninth houre till evening.

The names given are intensely problematic; firstly, this list does not match the previous list of kings (Bileth, Beliall, Asmoday, and Gaap). Amaymon is a higher order of king (the Emperors of Trithemius) than Gorson (Pursan and variants), and, probably, Gaap. Zimimar does not appear in the catalogues under that name, and is so far impossible to identify. It is therefore difficult to ascertain whether the text refers to the Great Kings (Oriens, Amaymon, Paimon, and Egyn) or to the kings serving them (as Bael for Oriens and so on), which are in any case closely linked to the Four Kings above who are usually simply invoked. For example, invoke Oriens and then conjure Bael. Since our sources envisage conjurations of the Four Kings, it is probably most expedient and likely to assume that all kings are intended. That only four are named – and those problematically – probably relates to Weyer's confessed tampering with the text, an interpretation I personally favour.

> Marquises may be bound from the ninth hour till compline, and
> from compline till the end of the day.

In the afternoon and evening is a clear enough reading of this instruction, awkward though the phrasing appears. On the other hand, if the operant was in holy orders, compline could indicate a pause, so the period given is not continuous.

More interesting is why Marquises should be listed directly after Kings, and why before Dukes, a very powerful rank in feudal terms? Again, it is useful to remove the supposed planetary considerations; second position earned them silver after gold, fobbing Dukes off with copper. This allows another look at them, reliant on internal considerations. Marquises appear in the Spirit Council, as do Dukes which follow. They also relate to very different times of day, with Marquises being by far the closest to the night of any rank mentioned. This suggests Marquises and Dukes may well be equal in status and alike in function, applicable at different times.

> Dukes may be bound from the first hour till noon; clear weather
> is to be observed.

For the entire morning; a period overlapping with both Kings and Presidents but not Marquises.

> Prelates may be bound in any hour of the day.

It would follow from the hypothesis given earlier that there would be a specific Prelate appropriate to the day.

> Knights from day dawning, till sun rising; or from evensong, till the sun set.

These timings suggest a connection with Dukes and Marquises as their superiors. This could well accord with a flexibility of timing suitable to the 'lesser operation' hypothesis.

> A President may not be bound in any hour of the day, unless the King, whom he obeys be invoked; nor in the shutting of the evening.

In other words, Presidents are conjured only when their Kings have been invoked – see above – and are not to be retained until the evening. Their presence on the Spirit Council is nigh overwhelming, and they may only be called when their King has been invoked. That stages of a hierarchical process of higher ranking intermediary spirits is intended is inescapable. How this integrates with the timings of the other ranks is where the subtlety resides; the devil, as they say, is in the detail.

> Counts or Earls may be bound at any hour of the day, so long as it is in the woods or fields, where men resort not.

At any time of day, in a quiet and secluded place; there appears to be no difference between the two ranks. It is worth noting that in general terms Marquises rule border kingdoms ('marches') and the title Duke has strong connotations of 'war leader'; thus both are of high degree and closer to the Kings. Counts (compare 'counties') are of lesser degree in feudal terms, their territories being peaceful ones of less military significance.

I now follow the example of the *Book of Offices* first list, and give the spirits in order of rank from the Weyer catalogue, the *Livre des Esperitz* and the *Book of Offices*, showing their affinities and occasional discrepancies. Note that *LdE* refers to princes where the *Goetia* has presidents, but is otherwise consistent with Weyer and so forth. This entire listing of course is secondary to that of the Lucifer, Belzebuth, Satan trinity and the Four Kings, and variations thereon.

Weyer Spirits by Rank	*Livre des Esperitz* 1 and 2	*Book of Offices* List 1 (with additions from unranked list 2 where obvious)
Kings	Kings	Kings
Bael	Veal/Beal	Baall
Bileth		Byleth
Buer	Gemen/Gemer	
Purson/Curson	Dicision/Diusion	Tersone/Gorsyar/Garsan Seson
Asmoday	Asmoday	Asmoday
Zagan	Zagon/Bugan	Uriell/Uriall (usually an angel!)
Belial	Brial/Vaal	Belial
[Gaap]		
Vine		
Balam		Barson
Decarabia/Carabia		Cambra
[Paimon]	Samon	Tamon? L.Carmeryn/ Cayenam?
		[Bealphares]
		Elyeth, Ebeyeth, Abech
		Harchase

Weyer Spirits by Rank	*Livre des Esperitz* 1 and 2	**Book of Offices** Lists 1 (with additions from unranked list 2 where obvious)
Presidents	= Princes	= Presidents
[Gaap]	Coap/Caap	–
Marbas	Barbas/Barthas	Barbas/Corbas
Buer	Gemen (King)	
Otis	Artis	Ogya
Morax		Formecones
Glasyabolas	Carmola	Gloolas. Neophon.
Forcas	Parcas	Forcas. Foras. Partas. Lewteffar aka Falcas (much elaborated). Annobath much resembles him.
Malphas	Malphares	Mallapar
Amy	–	Hanar, Tamor/Chamor
Haagenti (K.Zagan as President)	Dragon	–
Valac	–	Doolas
Ose	Oze	Oze
Pruslas	Bulfas	Suffales

It is sufficiently clear from this that the terms 'President' and 'Prince' are equivalent; this greatly clarifies some details of the *Goetia* catalogue as well as general practical principles underlying the hierarchy across the genre.

DUCAL TABLE

Weyer Dukes	Livre des Esperitz 1 and 2	Book of Offices Lists 1 and 2
Agares	Agarat	Acharos/Ahuras
Pruslas	Bulfas	Suffales
Barbatos	Batal/Barbas	Barbates/Barbares
Gusoin	Gazon	
Bathin	Machin	Marshiones
Abigor	Abugor	Allogar/Algor
Valefor		
Zepar		Hooab/Semp
Bune	Bune	
Berith	Berteth	Berith
[Astaroth]	Estor	Astaroth
Vepar/Separ		
Procell		Porax?
Murmur		
Focalor		
Gomory	—	Gemyem. Carmeyn or Cayenam. Gemon.
Amduscias		
Aym		Pathyn
Vapula		Moyle?
Flauros	Flanos	
Allocer		Lechor
Vuall		Reyall

Additional notes on 'Princes' in the Weyer and *Goetia* catalogues follow here. Note that the rank of Prince as such does not appear in the timing rules of these catalogues.

Weyer Spirits by Rank	Livre des Esperitz 1 and 2	Book of Offices Lists 1 and 2
Princes [sic]		
Amon? Marquis and perhaps a Prince	Marquis Amon	
Ipos. Earl and Prince	Count Vipos	
Sitri	Marquis Bitur	
[Gaap]	Prince Coap	
Orobas		
Stolas	Marquis Distolas	Mistolas (no rank)
[Vassago]		Marquis Usagoo

Weyer Spirits by Rank	Livre des Esperitz 1 and 2	Book of Offices Lists 1 and 2
Marquises	Marquises	
Amon	Amon	Amon (no rank)
Oray		
Cerberus	Cerbere	
Forneus		
Ronove		
Marchosias	Margotias	
Sabnacke/Salmac	Salmatis	
Shax	Deas/Drap (Duke)	Skor (duplicated as King and K.Prz.) Star.
Gamigin		Marquis Sogan/Sogom
Orias		
Andras		
Andrealphus	Andralfus Tudiras-Hoho	
Cimeries		Sowrges
Phoenix	Fenix	
Decarabia (King and Count in Weyer, Marquis in Goetia)		Possibly Barton aka Bartyn, duke.
[Vassago, Prince]		Usagoo

Weyer Spirits by Rank	Livre des Esperitz 1 and 2	Book of Offices Lists 1 and 2
Counts or Earls	Counts	Counts or Earls
Barbatos ('also a Duke')		Viscount (and Lord) Barbates/Barbares; probably Earl Loonex
Botis (also a President)		
Morax (President)		Earl Goorox
Ipos/Ayperos (Prince. sic)	Count Vipos	
Ronove (also a Marquis)		
Furfur	Count Furfur	
Murmur (also a Duke)		
Raum or Raim		
Halphas		
Vine (King)		
Saleos		
	Count Dam aka Jain	
		Geyll
		Deydo/Deyoo
		Royne
		Bryman or Mycirion
		Lyeonell

THE SPIRITS: BAEL TO GLASYABOLAS

Comparative analysis of Weyer's first eighteen; Weyer's listing is chosen for convenience rather than implying any canonical status.

BAEL... FIRST KING OF THE EAST

Weyer's spirits	Livre des Esperitz (list)	Livre des Esperitz (catalog)	Book of Offices (2 catalogs)	Grand Grimoire
Bael, Baell	Veal	Beal	Bael, Baall	Bael, first of 18 'subordinate' spirits

BAËL, JACQUES COLLIN DE PLANCY'S *DICTIONNAIRE INFERNAL*

BAEL, MATHERS' *GOETIA*

The major King among the spirits; Scot's text below, which has a pleasing period flavour, gives many of the essentials concerning Bael, Beal or Baal, a King of spirits who appears in several catalogues of spirits, invariably in first place.

> Baell. Their first and principal King (which is of the power of the east) is called Baëll who when he is conjured up, appeareth with three heads; the first, like a tode; the second, like a man; the third, like a cat. He speaketh with a hoarse voice, he maketh a man go invisible, he hath under his obedience and rule sixtie and six legions of divels.

The *Livre des Esperitz* specifies his immediate superior to be Oriens, and probably this has been translated as East in other forms of the catalogue. The alternative Four Kings in Weyer and the *Goetia* is thus directly contradicted by previous texts, including the English *Book of Offices*. This does not diminish the possible importance of these alternatives; it is undoubtedly easier however to consider the whole family of texts with the primary Oriens group assumed.

To resume, Bael or Baal appears in first place and with similar text in Weyer, Scot, the *Livre des Esperitz* and the *Goetia of Solomon*. He is also first listed among the spirits of the East in the *Book of Offices* more detailed catalogue. He is also first among eighteen subordinate spirits of the *Grand Grimoire* (following Weyer's listing, not the *Goetia*'s), and other confirmatory references abound. There is for example the 18th 'Secret' of *Liber De Angelis* (*Conjuring Spirits*, ed. Claire Fanger, p55), for 'Power over Demons'. This is a ritual of image-making for 'dominion over the demons and especially over Baal, who is their lord'.

Incidentally, references to image making in the spirit catalogues, explicit and implicit, are tolerably common. This particular rite has a close match (in *ms. B20*, cited and illustrated by Lecouteux) where the spirit in question is not Bael but Belial. An image of Belial is, perhaps obliquely, mentioned in the Scot and *Goetia* texts.

Baal's precedence, the sources clarify, is not over Eastern spirits alone. Simply put, he is the collective chief of the subordinate spirits. In this, as an Eastern King, he resembles Oriens, his Lord, who is the greatest among the Four Kings. Baal's precedence, after his superiors, is matched by Late Antique conceptions of the solar decans; the first of which was Lord of the rest, and the resemblance is apt. More extended discussion of these topics appears throughout the *Encyclopedia Goetica*. Baal of course was a name frequently associated with the Syrian or Chaldean sun god in Late Antiquity. His capacity as chief of all subordinates links him with key intermediary figures in several of the grimoires examined here. Whether this linkage is to the point of identity is moot; in any case 'Bael' like 'Oriens' is a title and as such can presumably be transferred.

The relations – to the point of identity – that exist between Oriens and Bael are expressed differently but nonetheless mirrored in the *Grand Grimoire*. Therein he is the first of three spirits under Lucifuge Rofocale (aka Sirachi, and variants), who in turn serves Lucifer. Careful readers will note the priority this gives him is retained in either case.

AGARES... First Duke of the East

Weyer's spirits	Livre des Esperitz (list and catalog)	Book of Offices 1st list	Book of Offices 2nd list	Others
Agares	Agarat	Acharos, Ahuras	Agaros	The second of 18 'subordinate' spirits in GG. The German *Honorius* appears to list him twice, as Agarus and Agerol.

Aguarès, from Jacques Collin de Plancy's *Dictionnaire Infernal*

Agares, Mathers' Goetia

Agares, Duke. Second spirit named in Weyer and *GoS* catalogues, a subordinate in the *Grand Grimoire*. He is the first Duke of the East, a spirit under Oriens. *Off* list 1 lists him as Acharos and Ahuras. *Off* list 2 has Agaros, again under Oriens; *LdE* has Agarat, the German *Honorius* Agarus and Agerol, duplicated. Scot's listing, drawn from Weyer, says of him:

> Agares. The first duke under the power of the east, is named Agares, he commeth up mildile in the likenes of a faire old man, riding upon a crocodile, and carrieng a hawke on his fist; hee teacheth presentlie all maner of toongs, he fetcheth backe all such as runne awaie, and maketh them runne that stand still; he overthroweth all dignities supernaturall and temporall, hee maketh earthquakes, and is of the order of vertues, having under his regiment thirtie one legions.

Note *the first Duke under the power of the East*. The first listing in *Off* also specifies that Acharos or Ahuras is a Duke and under the King of the East. From this and like references it is certain that this particular Duke is Eastern. From 'first' we are likely also intended to understand him to be senior to any other Eastern duke, which in turn may imply to dukes in general. This is important information in any projected reconstruction of the hierarchy in practice.

In the *Grand Grimoire* and related systems Agares is the second of three spirits under Lucifuge Rofocale, who answers to Lucifer.

MARBAS...

Weyer's spirits	Livre des Esperitz (list)	Livre des Esperitz (catalog)	Book of Offices 2nd list	Grand Grimoire
Marbas, Barbas	Barbas (prince)	Barthas	Barbas/ Corbas	GG's third spirit

MARBAS, MATHERS' GOETIA

Again drawing on Scot:

> Marbas, alias Barbas is a great president, and appeareth in the forme of a mightie lion; but at the commandement of a conjuror commeth up in the likenes of a man, and answereth fullie as touching anie thing which is hidden or secret: he bringeth diseases, and cureth them, he promoteth wisedome, and the knowledge of mechanicall arts, or handicrafts; he changeth men into other shapes, and under his presidencie or gouvernement are thirtie six legions of divels conteined.

Note how Presidency and Government are used as interchangeable terms here. In the *Book of Oberon* there are several (Lords and) Governors who we may assume to be equivalent to Presidents. Marbas aka Barbas is certainly a President, and on the Presidential Council with responsibilities for the Eastern jurisdiction.

In *Offices* again this spirit is located in the Eastern column and in third place, exactly as Weyer lists him. Likewise, in the *Grand Grimoire* Marbas is the third of three spirits under Lucifuge Rofocale.

PRUSLAS...

Weyer's spirits	Livre des Esperitz (list)	Livre des Esperitz (catalog)	Book of Offices (2 catalogs)	Grand Grimoire
Pruslas, Busas	Bulfas (prince)	Bulfas	Suffales	Pruslas is included in the *Grand Grimoire*, though missing from Scot and the *Goetia*.

PRUFLAS, FROM JACQUES COLLIN DE PLANCY'S *DICTIONNAIRE INFERNAL*

A Prince or Duke; while included in Weyer's catalogue, he was omitted somehow from Scot's text and consequently from the *Goetia*. This omission is among the strong indicators that the *Goetia* is partially reliant on the material in Scot, although it has other sources. Interestingly however, he is included with variant names in the earlier *Book of Offices* catalogue, as well as the *Livre de Esperitz*, which is also older, and which we quote here:

Bulfas is a great prince. His office is to make discords and battles, and when he is well constrained, he returns good response of that which one asks him; and has beneath him 36 legions.

In the *Grand Grimoire* and related systems Pruslas is the first of three spirits under Satanachia, second minister of Lucifer. His presence in the *Grand Grimoire* demonstrates its direct relations with Weyer, distinct from Scot and the *Goetia of Solomon* in England. The *Book of Offices*, which predates the Scot/GoS line, knows him as Suffales, a spirit under Oriens.

AMON...

Weyer's spirits	Livre des Esperitz (list)	Livre des Esperitz (catalog)	Book of Offices 2nd list	Others
Amon	Amon	Amon	Amon	Aamon GG Amon appears in *ms. Plut.89 Sup.38.* This may support Princely status.

AMON, FROM JACQUES COLLIN DE PLANCY'S *DICTIONNAIRE INFERNAL*

AMON, *PLUT.* 89

AMON, MATHERS' *GOETIA*

The description in Scot is as follows:

> Amon, or Aamon, is a great and mightie marques, and commeth
> abroad in the likenes of a woolfe, having a serpents taile,
> spetting out and breathing flames of fier; when he putteth on
> the shape of a man, he sheweth out dogs teeth, and a great head
> like to a mightie raven; he is the strongest prince of all other,
> and understandeth of all things past and to come, he procureth
> favor, and reconcileth both freends and foes, and ruleth fourtie
> legions of divels.

In the *Grand Grimoire* and related systems Amon is the second of
three spirits under Satanachia. The reference to a prince is possibly
generic (if all the spirits are princes, but only a Prince is a President). His
non-appearance in the Presidential Council should also be considered
in assessing this. Amon is also among the Eastern spirits in the *Book of
Offices*.

BARBATOS...

Weyer's spirits	Livre des Esperitz (list)	Livre des Esperitz (catalog)	Book of Offices 2 catalogues	Others
Barbatos	Batal	Barbas	1st: Barbates/ Barbares and a duplicate Barbates. 2nd Barbais	Barbatos GG. Barbarus *clm 849*

BARBATOS, FROM JACQUES COLLIN DE PLANCY'S *DICTIONNAIRE INFERNAL*

BARBATOS, MATHERS' *GOETIA*

Here I give Scot's description, with some necessary interpolated comments:

> Barbatos, a great countie or earle, and also a duke, he appeareth in Signo sagittarii sylvestris [in the form of an archer of the woods, NOT in the Sign of Sagittarius], with foure kings, which bring trumpets [not companies] and great troopes. He understandeth the singing of birds, the barking of dogs, the lowings of bullocks, and the voice of all living creatures. He detecteth treasures hidden by magicians and inchanters, and is of the order of vertues, which in part beare rule: he knoweth all things past, and to come, and reconcileth freends and powers; and governeth thirtie legions of divels by his authoritie.

In the *Grand Grimoire* and related systems Barbatos is the third of three spirits under Satanachia. Earl is simply used in the text as an alternative to Count, which is the original term. The *Book of Offices* repeats his entry, once with the correct translation (forest archer), then again with the 'Sagittarius' reading. This suggests collation from more than one source. It places him in the East with several other spirits from this part of Weyer's listing. He is, moreover, a member of the Presidential Council. Possibly Barbas and Barbatos were once the same spirit; this cannot now be ascertained. This would perhaps explain why there is one more spirit governing the East than the other directions, but they have undergone separate evolutions and must be considered distinct.

Barbatos is very likely identical with Baraborat, an angel of the East ruling on Wednesday according to the *Heptameron*. This grimoire had a huge influence and accounts for a few of the names in this directory, as well as supplying incantations for the *Goetia of Solomon*. The Eastern attribution certainly rings true with the information we have of Barbatos.

BUER...

Weyer's spirits	Livre des Esperitz (list)	Livre des Esperitz (catalog)	Book of Offices (2 catalogs)	Others
Buer	Gemen (King)	Gemer	Unidentified	Buer GG Heneral in the German *Honorius*, Heramael in the GV which includes material omitted in mss supposed by some to be precursors.

BUER, FROM JACQUES COLLIN DE PLANCY'S *DICTIONNAIRE INFERNAL*

BUER, MATHERS' *GOETIA*

Scot's text is as follows:

> Buer is a great president, and is seene in this signe [*]; he
> absolutelie teacheth philosophie morall and naturall, and also
> logicke, and the vertue of herbes: he giveth the best familiars,
> he can heale all diseases, speciallie of men, and reigneth over
> fiftie legions.

From this the *Goetia* somehow arrived at:

> *Buer, a Great President. He appeareth in Sagittary, and that is his
> shape when the Sun is there...*

Evidently astrologically oriented editors in the past have made too
much of the word 'sign' in various places in the catalogue. It is translated
from the Latin 'signo'; which can also, as it does here, mean image or
form. Also, while not in Scot's text, Weyer's asterisk represents a blank
in the text, that is, the description is missing. This occurs also with
Decarabia, which is badly bowdlerised in the *Goetia*; with Aym, only
part of the description is missing, again marked by an asterisk, again
misinterpreted in the *Goetia*.

A President, Buer was the first of the spirits of the *Goetia* my research
identified with a spirit of the *Grimorium Verum*. This breakthrough
occurred via the German *Honorius*, where he is listed as Heneral. This
alias is among the indicators that the spirit names of the GV have
enjoyed wider distribution. In both *Wellcome MS 4669* and *Lansdowne
MS 1202*, supposed by some to be precursor mss of the GV, all details
concerning Heramael are omitted. The GV however gives them correctly,
as can be substantiated via 1) the description of Heneral in the German
Honorius, and 2) Buer in the Weyer/*Goetia* catalogue once the identity
is established; plainly it cannot have done this had it depended on the
manuscripts supposed to have preceded it.

The name as it appears in the *Livre des Esperitz* looks close to GV
and German forms (Gemer being phonetically similar to Hener, and
possessing the 'm' in Heramael. Forms of names in *Honorius*, several
French grimoires and their dependent texts preserve variant names at

least as old as those known from Weyer and associated Germanic and English traditions. The implications regarding the GV are plain; so far as the early spirit catalogue is concerned it is closer to a primary source than a derivative or variant text.

In the *Grand Grimoire* and related systems Buer is the first of three spirits under Agliarept, first minister of Belzebuth. He has yet to be identified in the *Oberon* stemma. His is clearly an important role, as a President with significant practical gifts; further exploration promises reward.

GUSOYN...

Weyer's spirits	Livre des Esperitz (list)	Livre des Esperitz (catalog)	Others
Gusoyn	Gazon	Gazon	Gusoyn GG. 'Johann' GH. Cason clm 849

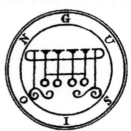

GUISON, MATHERS' GOETIA

Gusoin is a great duke, and a strong, appearing in the forme of a [Seneschalus], he answereth all things, present, past, and to come, expounding all questions. He reconcileth freendship, and distributeth honours and dignities, and ruleth over fourtie legions of divels.

Scot

The clm 849 MS clarifies the inexplicable 'xenophilus' of the Goetia as a garbling of 'seneschal': a senior knightly officer; a king's most trusted man; a royal steward, and such like. The 'Johann' of the German Honorius compares with the mangling of Andromalius as 'Andrew Malchus' elsewhere.

In the Grand Grimoire Gusoyn is the second of three spirits under Agliarept; who answers to Belzebuth.

BOTIS...

Weyer's spirits	Livre des Esperitz (list)	Livre des Esperitz (catalog)	Book of Offices (1st catalog)	Others
Botis, Otis	Artis (prince)	Artis	Ogya	Botis, GG. Artis, German *Honorius*. Otius, *clm 849*

BOTIS, MATHERS' GOETIA

Botis, otherwise Otis, a great president and an earle he commeth foorth in the shape of an ouglie viper, and if he put on humane shape, he sheweth great teeth, and two hornes, carrieng a sharpe sword in his hand: he giveth answers of things present, past, and to come, and reconcileth friends, and foes, ruling sixtie legions.

Scot

Botis – a President and Earl – also appears in the German *Honorius* under a slightly different name, and a still different name in the *Book of Offices*. It is probably significant that he and Buer (see above) share the same rank. He only appears, so far as can be established, in the first of the catalogues of the *Book of Offices*, which gives no indication of directionality.

In the *Grand Grimoire* Botis is the third of three spirits under Agliarept.

BATHYM...

Weyer's spirits	Livre des Esperitz (list)	Livre des Esperitz (catalog)	Book of Offices (2 catalogs)	Others
Bathym (Bathin), Mathim	Machin	Machin	Marshioness Maxayn	Bathim, GG. Machin in German *Honorius*. GV's Trimasael, (again the supposed 'mss precursors' omit details present in the GV)

BATHIM, MATHERS' *GOETIA*

Bathin, sometimes called Mathim, a great duke and a strong, he is seene in the shape of a verie strong man, with a serpents taile, sitting on a pale horsse, understanding the vertues of hearbs and pretious stones, transferring men suddenlie from countrie to countrie, and ruleth thirtie legions of divels.

Scot

A Duke, like Buer/Heramael Bathym appears under a slightly different name in the German *Honorius*; he can also be identified in both the *Livre des Esperitz* and the *Book of Offices*. Like him too his name and sigil appears in the supposed GV 'precursors', but with the details correctly given in the GV omitted.

Another, more magical, connection between them exists. The GV names four spirits under Satanachia – all lacking details in the *Wellcome* and *Lansdowne* forms – and both spirits are part of this group. The two spirits appearing between these names in the Weyer catalogue and elsewhere do not appear to be the other two. Nevertheless, Heramael and Trimasael are the first spirits of the GV to be identified with spirits outside the catalogue, other than the major chiefs. They are thus responsible ultimately for this entire comparative treatise, and vindicate my thesis regarding the notorious French grimoire and its importance.

In the *Book of Offices* he is listed under Oriens in the East. In the *Grand Grimoire* he is the first of three spirits under Fleruty, a minister of Belzebuth.

PURSAN...

Weyer's spirits	Livre des Esperitz (list)	Livre des Esperitz (catalog)	Book of Offices 1st catalog	Book of Offices 2nd catalog	Others
Pursan (Purson) Curson	Dicision	Diusion	Tersone/ Fersone. Gorsyar. Garsan/ Garsone. Corsone.	Seson. Gordoser.	Curson, clm 849. Gordonizer, Sloane 3824. etc.

PURSON, MATHERS' GOETIA

Purson, alias Curson, a great king, he commeth foorth like a man with a lions face, carrieng a most cruell viper, and riding on a beare; and before him go alwaies trumpets, he knoweth things hidden, and can tell all things present, past, and to come: he bewraieth treasure, he can take a bodie either humane or aierie; he answereth truelie of all things earthlie and secret, of the divinitie and creation of the world, and bringeth foorth the best familiars; and there obeie him two and twentie legions of divels, partlie of the order of vertues, and partlie of the order of thrones.

Scot

Undoubtedly a great king with extensive mentions in the literature, Pursan remains somewhat mysterious. His antique roots, if any, are unclear. At one point Weyer's text suggests he is king of the South, but this formulation is suspect. He is extensively duplicated in the *Book of Offices*, and under a variety of ranks. In the first ranked listing Tersone is a King, as are Gorsyar and Garsan; Corsone however is a Count. More importantly, he appears twice in the second listing, which attributes spirits to the directions. Here Seson is named as might be expected, in the East; related to the appearance of Purson in Weyer's 1st 18, and to the form of the name Purson, Curson, Tersone, and so forth. Gordoser however – a major variant of the name, akin to Gorsyar and other forms – is listed in the West, under Paymon. Although there is not much apparent duplication in the second listing, there may be some sort of pattern with those that do occur. One could think of these spirits as functioning on more than one path of the crossroads.

In *Sloane 3824* the variant Gordonizer is used when discussing his role in the Presidential Council. With so many variants for this spirit's name (in *Offices* List 1 alone), this particular identification took longer than most, but is firm. Though approaching from another angle, JHP made the same identification. In the *Grand Grimoire* Pursan is the second of three spirits under Fleruty, second minister of Belzebuth.

ABIGOR...

Weyer's spirits	Livre des Esperitz (list)	Livre des Esperitz (catalog)	Book of Offices (2 catalogs)	Others
Eligor, Abigor	Abugor	Abugor	Allogar, Algor,	Eligor/Eligos GG Jilbagor, German *Honorius*. Alugor, *clm 849*

ABIGOR, FROM JACQUES COLLIN DE PLANCY'S *DICTIONNAIRE INFERNAL*

ELIGOS, MATHERS' GOETIA

Eligor, alias Abigor, is a great duke, and appeereth as a goodlie knight, carrieng a lance, an ensigne, and a scepter: he answereth fullie of things hidden, and of warres, and how souldiers should meete: he knoweth things to come, and procureth the favour of lords and knights, governing sixtie legions of divels.

Scot

Abigor appears under this name or as Eligor in the Weyer, Scot, *Goetia* cluster. In *Book of Offices* List One, he is Allogar, in List Two Algor, a spirit under Oriens. The *Livre des Esperitz* has Abugor; the German *Honorius* Jilbagor. Like all the first 18 spirits in the Weyer list he appears in the *Grand Grimoire* and its derivatives; named there as Eligos, the third of three spirits under Fleruty. An important spirit, he is among the Presidential Councillors.

ORAY...

Weyer's spirits	Book of Offices 1ˢᵗ Catalog	Others
Oray, Leraie	Barsy	Loray, GG. Berci, *Sloane 3853.*

> Leraie, alias Oray, a great marquesse, shewing himselfe in the
> likenesse of a galant archer, carrieng a bowe and a quiver, he
> is author of all battels, he dooth putrifie all such wounds as
> are made with arrows by archers, Quos optimos objicit tribus
> diebus, and he hath regiment over thirtie legions.
>
> Scot

The Latin, which is defective, was left untranslated in Scot. Joseph
Peterson's identification of him with 'Barsy, a great ruler and a captain'
in *Oberon*'s first listing is admirable. In *Sloane 3853* too he finds Berci – a
captayne. This ms tells us he is 'a great revler', but perhaps ruler is meant.
So too it has 'a quiver of Iroz', undoubtedly 'arrows' as Joseph indicates.
Agares is referred to as the 'first Captain of the East' in *Sloane 3824*, so
Captain possibly equals Duke.

In the *Grand Grimoire* Loray is the first of three spirits under
Sargatanas, a minister of Astaroth.

VALEFAR...

Weyer's spirits	Others
Valefar/Malephar	Valefar, GG Brufor, *Armadel?*

VALEFOR, MATHERS' GOETIA

Valefar, alias Malephar, is a strong duke, comming foorth in the shape of a lion, and the head of a theefe, he is verie familiar with them to whom he maketh himself acquainted, till he hath brought them to the gallowes, and ruleth ten legions.

Scot

In the *Grand Grimoire* Valefar is the second of three spirits under Sargatanas, first minister of Astaroth. Most of our sources remain quiet concerning him; a spirit named Brufor in the *Grimoire of Armadel* has a character much like his. Beguiling though this is, it provides no further leads.

MORAX...

Weyer's spirits	Book of Offices 1st list	Others
Morax/Foraii	Formecones, Goorox/ Goorax.	Foraii/Faraii GG Corax, *Sloane 3853*

MORAX, MATHERS' GOETIA

Morax, alias Foraii, a great earle and a president, he is seene like a bull, and if he take unto him a mans face, he maketh men wonderfull cunning in astronomie, and in all the liberall sciences: he giveth good familiars and wise, knowing the power and vertue of hearbs and stones which are pretious, and ruleth thirtie six legions.

Scot

In the *Grand Grimoire* Morax is the third of three spirits under Sargatanas. *Oberon*, often parsimonious, reduces his legions to 30, while *Sloane 3853* increases them to 90. Both reckon him an Earl. His double in *Offices*, Formecones, is a Prince (President) and his legions match those in Weyer.

IPOS...

Weyer's spirits	Livre des Esperitz (list)	Livre des Esperitz (catalog)	Book of Offices (2 catalogs)	Others
Ipos	Vipos	Vipos	Unidentified	Ayperos, GG

IPOS, MATHERS' GOETIA

Ipos, alias Ayporos, is a great earle and a prince, appeering in the shape of an angell, and yet indeed more obscure and filthie than a lion, with a lions head, a gooses feet, and a hares taile: he knoweth things to come and past, he maketh a man wittie, and bold, and hath under his jurisdiction thirtie six legions.

Scot

Not so far identified in *Off*; in the *Grand Grimoire* Ayperos is the first of three spirits under Nebiros, a minister of Astaroth.

CERBERUS...

Weyer's spirits	*Livre des Esperitz* (list)	*Livre des Esperitz* (catalog)	*Book of Offices* (2 catalogs)	Others
Naberus, (Naberius), Cerberus	Cerbere	Cerbere	Unidentified	Naberus in the *Grand Grimoire*. References to Cerberus abound in the *PGM*, and his syncretic identity with Anubis should not be overlooked.

CERBERÈ, FROM JACQUES COLLIN DE PLANCY'S *DICTIONNAIRE INFERNAL*

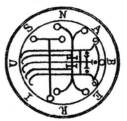

NABERIUS, MATHERS' *GOETIA*

Naberius, alias Cerberus, is a valiant marquesse, shewing himselfe in the forme of a crowe, when he speaketh with a hoarse voice: he maketh a man amiable and cunning in all arts, and speciallie in rhetorike, he procureth the losse of prelacies and dignities: nineteene legions heare and obeie him.

Scot

Scot's rendering 'Naberius' is probably in error; Weyer has Naberus. In the *Grand Grimoire* Cerberus aka Naberus is the second of three spirits under Nebiros, whose name much resembles his. Frustratingly, while present in the *LdE* he is not apparently known to the *Book of Offices*.

His likely connection with Nebiros/Nebirots either as identical or an emanation, is one of the important mysteries of the grimoire cycle (see *GV, GG, GH*). An entire chapter was devoted to him in *Geo*, which is unlikely to be exhaustive.

GLASYALABOLAS...

Weyer's spirits	Livre des Esperitz (list)	Livre des Esperitz (catalog)	Book of Offices (2 catalogs)	Grand Grimoire
Glassy- Labolas, Caacrinolas, Caasimolar	Carmola (prince)	Carmola	Gloolas, Neophon	Glasyabolas

GLASYA-LABOLAS, MATHERS' *GOETIA*

Glasya Labolas, alias Caacrinolaas, or Caassimolar, is a great president, who commeth foorth like a dog, and hath wings like a griffen, he giveth the knowledge of arts, and is the captaine of all mansleiers: he understandeth things present and to come, he gaineth the minds and love of freends and foes, he maketh a man go invisible, and hath the rule of six and thirtie legions.

Scot

A President, with all that implies; this spirit has a variety of aliases, clarifying which has operative implications of note. Weyer calls him Glasya Labolas, alias Caacrinolaas, or Caassimolar.

The latter of Weyer's aliases eases our way to identifying him with Prince Carmola in the *LdE*. *Offices'* King or Prince Gloolas in the first listing has the same appearance and the same powers; again there are some phonetic similarities.

Under Oriens in the second listing is Neophon; here there is no resemblance of name, but a very similar list of powers and canine form. Neophon is evidently the Niopheyn of the Presidential Council, of whom we have far more knowledge once this identity with Glasyabolas is established. That this is the case is clear, following the description in *Offices*, according to which he has *power to tell all things that have or will be, and indeed all secrets; gives the favour of great men, appeaseth the emnity of foes, gives dignity, worship and riches, and appeareth like a dog.*

As Glasyabolas he also appears in the *Grand Grimoire*'s spirit catalogue, which of course duplicates Weyer's first 18 (starting with Baal and Agares). Therein Glasyabolas is the third of three spirits under Nebiros, a minister of Astaroth. The relation of Glasyabolas with the Eastern part of the hierarchy, in both Continental and English forms of the tradition, is thus systematically confirmed.

ADDITIONAL SPIRITS

TO BRING this part of our discussion to a satisfactory conclusion involves returning to the *Grimorium Verum*. As mentioned previously this grimoire has an initial hierarchy resembling that of the *Grand Grimoire*. In addition, it details other spirits important to itself and this discussion. Unlike the spirit catalogues above, the subordinate spirits in this second listing are not evenly distributed among the deputies in the least:

Deputy ruling	Spirit Subordinates
Satanachia	45 unnamed demons, also said 54, with these 4 chiefs: Sergutthy; Heramael; Trimasael; Sustugriel.
Agliarept and Tarihimal	Elelogap
Nebirots via Hael and Sergulath	Proculo, Haristum, Brulefer, Pentagnony, Aglasis, Sidragosam, Minoson, Bucon

It will be noted how Nebirots, by having two deputies of his own here, resembles the Chiefs of the preceding groups. As will be detailed further on, two of the spirits under Satanachia can be readily identified with spirits of the *Goetia*, Weyer and Scot, facilitated by their aliases in the German *Honorius*. A conjuration associated wholly with this grouping and involving precisely 18 names was referred to earlier (under Saturday in the Seven Days section).

Before moving on, note as well that – depending on the edition – Satanachia is said to have 45 or 54 demons beneath him. Since 54+18=72, these are just conceivably the remaining demons of Weyer, Scot and *The Goetia of Solomon the King*. This would bring the *Grand Grimoire* demons into a yet more intimate relationship with the *Verum* hierarchy. Perhaps more significant however is the reference to fifty-four demons in the *Speculum Astronomiae* of Albertus Magnus. This C13th work underpins much later thinking, in and out of the Church, concerning astrology and by extension magic; it was in fact one of the first books on occult subjects read by Cornelius Agrippa.

To clarify this important reference and provide context, Albertus is at pains to rid astrology of "necromantic" elements. Image-making, and other "necromantic" practices then connected to Electional Astrology, was an area of particular concern to him. Three kinds of images are discussed; the most abominably "necromantic" are images of the Lunar Mansions. These have Greek, Babylonian, and Arab connections, and diabolic or not there is certainly nothing Christian about them. These images he says are served by "fifty four angels who are probably really demons". Significantly one late MS of the work changes 54 to 72. This adjustment likely relates to the later idea of 72 spirits in the *Goetia*. Spirit catalogues in general have affinities with ancient ideas about the decans. This aside, a decan-based limit of 72 spirits appears to be a conceit of early modern English grimoire makers, one without support from earlier Continental sources. The number may well have been force fitted to line up the spirits with the angels of the Shemhamphorash, an association which is largely unsupported – indeed contradicted – by early Continental manuscript traditions. Since the order in which the spirits appear in the *Goetia* is an innovation, such an association with cabalistic angels has to be of later vintage than the widely dispersed catalogues of spirits considered here. An ancient relation to the decans is another matter, and resurfacing of such a background is to be expected.

SUMMARY

To recap, 18 is an important number in the organisation of the *Grimorium Verum* and the *Grand Grimoire*. The spirit lists outlined above and the eighteen spirits in the incantation speak of this. So too, the first 18 spirits of Weyer's catalogue are a very stable grouping in several other texts. Note also that 72 and 54 appear as totals of spirits of various hierarchies, and both these numbers divide by 18. These are all indicators of a long established tradition, now barely visible, in which an extended hierarchy of spirits with known identities and inter-relations was assumed in the grimoire literature. Comparative work across the genre therefore has plenty to engage with, both in terms of identities and of organisational principles.

THE
SPIRIT CATALOGUES
PART TWO

LBS AND BEYOND

THE SPIRIT CATALOGUE in Weyer, transmitted via Scot and extended and rearranged in the *Goetia of Solomon*, has substantial connections with spirit hierarchies to be found elsewhere. As seen, the 'subordinate spirits' of the *Grand Grimoire* exactly duplicates the first 18 spirits from Weyer's list, which are also the first 18 of *Livre des Esperitz*. *Le Livre des Esperitz* contains a list and a longer, differing catalogue of spirits and their feudal rankings. While not identical there are obviously close relations between this catalogue and Weyer's, and comparison clarifies a good deal. In *Le Livre des Esperitz*, unlike the *Goetia of Solomon*, the chief spirits (Lucifer, Belzebut, and Satan) and Four Kings (Orient, Poymon, Amoymon, and Equi) are listed first. Both the list and the catalogue differ in other respects from Weyer and the GoS; this extends to some extra spirits as well as some omissions. Some of the spirits are known from other sources, although their aliases have obscured some of the equivalences. These include the *Grimorium Verum* and a mangled but useful German MS of *Honorius*, as well as MS *clm 849* and elsewhere.

Another important and little considered text is *ms. Plut.89 Sup.38*. This text also has a catalogue with sigils, representing a variant tradition from the *Goetia*. While many of the demons therein do not obviously match up with the *Goetia* and its immediate predecessor texts, there are many recognisable figures, chiefly superior spirits, who do. So do others who research-driven magicians are nowadays recognising as important 'deputies' of these superiors. In short, this manuscript includes: Lucifer, Belzabuth, Astarot, Oriens, Amaymon, Paimon, Egin; these names are grouped together. In addition, Bilet, Hoel [Hael?], Aziel, Amon, Andaras [Andras?], Balperit, Liridam [Luridan?], Berit, and Belial are found. Other affinities with 'our' grimoires include a striking example among its various sigils of Lucifer, closely resembling those attributed in the GV.

The *clm 849* spirits are interesting as having obvious relations to Weyer's text. The short list includes a spirit not appearing in Weyer or its derivative texts such as the *Goetia*, but which can be found elsewhere. They are worth listing here ahead of larger tables.

Jake Stratton-Kent   117

SELECTED SIGILS FROM MS. PLUT.89 SUP.38

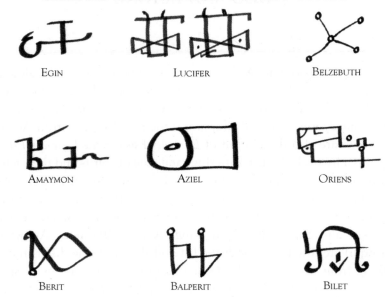

EGIN LUCIFER BELZEBUTH

AMAYMON AZIEL ORIENS

BERIT BALPERIT BILET

CLM *849* COMPARED WITH WEYER

clm 849	Weyer	clm 849	Weyer
Duke Barbarus*	Barbatos	Pres. Volac	Valac
Duke Cason*	Gusoin	Duke Gaeneron	(Paymon) Gomory (these spirits are so much alike it is difficult to see which is intended in various spirit lists).
Count Otius*	Otis, Artis	Marquis Tvueries	Cimeries
King Curson*	Curson etc	Pres. Hanni	Amy
Duke Alugor*	Abigor etc	Marquis Sucax	Not apparent in Weyer, *Scot* or the *Goetia*, but present in both *Offices* and LdE.
Prince Taob	Goap		

Note that Duke Barbarus, duke Cason, count Otius, king Curson and duke Alugor represent approximately half of the *clm 849* group, are listed consecutively and are also in Weyer's 1st 18.

Pandemonium: A Discordant Concordance of Diverse Spirit Catalogues

THE SPIRITS OF THE *LIVRE DES ESPERITZ*

THE OLDEST KNOWN substantial catalogue fully within this tradition, the *Book of Spirits* (*Livre des Esperitz*, LdE) overlaps with the Weyer list substantially, matching it spirit for spirit in the first eighteen cases. This justifies the assumption that the order of Weyer's first 18 is 'canonical' in this tradition. The catalogue is supplemented by a preliminary list of spirits and their ranks; both have to be considered as the contents are not identical. As can be seen, the table requires 54 compartments, which is 18x3.

Livre des Esperitz catalogue	*Livre des Esperitz* list
Lucifer	Lucifer
Belzebut	Belzebut
Satan	Satan
Orient (East)	Orient
Poymon (West)	Poymon
Amoymon (South)	Amoymon
Equi (North)	———
King Beal	King Veal
Duke Agarat	Duke Agarat
Prince Barthas	Prince Barbas
Prince Bulfas	Prince Bulfas
Marquis Amon	Marquis Amon
Prince Barbas	Prince Batal
King Gemer	King Gemen
Duke Gazon	Duke Gazon
Duke Artis	Prince Artis
Duke Machin	Duke Machin
King Diusion	King Dicision

THE SPIRITS OF THE *LIVRE DES ESPERITZ* (2)

Livre des Esperitz catalogue	*Livre des Esperitz* list
Duke Abugor	Duke Abugor
Count Vipos	Count Vipos
Marquis Cerbere	Marquis Cerbere
Prince Carmola	Prince Carmola
	Duke Estor
Marquis Salmatis	
Prince Coap	Prince Coap
Duke Drap	Duke Deas
King Asmoday	King Asmoday
Prince Caap (duplicated, see Coap)	
Duke Bune	
Marquis Bitur	Marquis Bitur
Duke Lucubar	
King Bugan	King Zagon
	Prince Dragon
Prince Parcas	Prince Parcas
	Duke Gorsin
Duke Flavos	Duke Flanos

THE SPIRITS OF THE *LIVRE DES ESPERITZ* (3)

Livre des Esperitz catalogue	*Livre des Esperitz* list
King Vaal	King Brial
Marquis Fenix	Marquis Fenix
Marquis Distolas	Marquis Distolas
Duke Berteth	Duke Beal
Count Dam	
Count Furfur	
Prince Forcas (duplicated, see Parcas)	Prince Forcas
Prince Malpharas	
	Count Furfur
	Marquis Margotias
Duke Gorsay	
King Samon	
Marquis Tudiras Hoho*	Marquis Andraflus
Marquis Ose	Prince Ose
Marquis Ducay	Marquis Lucay
Duke Bucal	Duke Pucel
	Count Jayn
	Duke Suralet

Tu diras is a Spanish term meaning 'you decide', likely an editor's comment over an undecipherable name or some such.

THE BOOK OF OFFICES

THE SPIRITS OF THE FIRST LIST, WITH RANKS

King. Terson (Pursan etc)	K. Garsan (duplicates Pursan)	D. Amada	E Barbares (2)	Knight? Pamelons, Paynelon
K. Elyeth (Abech above)	K. Tamon	D. Barton (possibly Decarabia)	Lord and Gov Annobath (Furcas, an important identification)	Kt. (Capt?) Gemon (another Gomory?)
K. Harchase	K and President. Darbas, Carbas	D. Allogor (Abigor etc)	L. Gemmos	Kt. Leban
K. Gorsyar (duplicates Pursan)	K.Prz Ogya (Otis)	D. Globa	L. Ansoryor or Antyor (maybe a further Furcas)	Kt. Doodal
K. Skor (Shax)	K.Prz Skor(3)	D. Marshiones (Bathim, Machin etc)	L. Noocar	Kt. Geenex
K. Garsan (duplicates Pursan)	K.Prz Drewchall	D. Bartyn (2)	Prelate Boal or Boall (similar to Allocer)	Capt. Coryx
K. Tamon	K.Prz.. Gloolas (Glassyabolas)	D. Kayne (Raum)	L Aron, Aran	[Mosacus]
K and President. Darbas, Carbas	President Forcase (Forcas etc)	D. Rewseyn	(M Capt and Gov) Iambex	[King Oberon]
K.Prz Ogya (Otis)	Prz.Coolor (Valac)	D. Gemyem (Gomory)	Gov or M. Fewrayne	[Bilgall]

K.Prz **Skor**(2)	Prz.Kewboo	Duke and Marquis Triblex	L Carmeryn/ Cayenam (a 2nd Paymon/ Gomory figure?)	[Myeob etc Sibyls]
K.Prz Drewchall	Prz.Hanar (Amy)	Earl Loonex (similar Barbatos)	L. Mathias	Knight? Pamelons, Paynelon
K.Prz..Gloolas (Glassyabolas)	Prz.Hooab (Zepar)	M. Moyle (similar Vapula)	Ruler Oorex	Kt. Gemon (another Gomory?)
President Forcase (Forcas etc)	Prz.Doolas (Valac)	E. Geyll	Ruler Mageyne	Kt. Leban
Prz.Coolor (Valac)	Prz. Formecones (Morax)	E. Deydo/ Deyoo	Ruler Gasyaxe	Kt. Doodal
Prz.Kewboo	Prz.Tamor or Chamor (Amy)	M. Sogan/ Sogom (Gamigin)	Ruler and captain Barsy	Kt. Geenex
King. Terson (Pursan etc)	Prz.Lewteffar or Falcas (Furcas etc, much elaborated)	E. Royne	R. Bartax	Capt. Coryx
K. Elyeth (Abech above)	Prz.Dyelagoo	M. Sowrges (Cimeries)	M. Usagoo (Vassago)	[Mosacus]
K. Harchase	Prz.Barbaryes	E. Bryman or Mycioron	Knight Gyell	[King Oberon]
K. Gorsyar (duplicates Pursan)	Prz.Porax (probably Procell)	Lord and Gt Viscount Barbates, Barbares (Barbatos)	Count Lyeonell	[Bilgall]
K. Skor (Shax)	Duke Acharos, Aharus (Agares)	E. Goorox	C. Corsone (Pursan)	[Mycob etc Sibyls]

Approximately 12 of these can be identified with spirits in Weyer's 1st 18; 8 in the 2nd, 15 including several duplicates in the 3rd and only 3 from the remnant. Spellings follow Hockley; hence some slight differences from *Oberon*.

Pandemonium: A Discordant Concordance of Diverse Spirit Catalogues

The second listing is very important, as it provides much more detailed information concerning which King rules which spirits. In particular, it tells us who their sub-kings and presidents are. Vassago, not in Weyer but present in the *Goetia*, can be identified here. While not definitive, this appearance suggests the *Goetia* had a relationship with English versions of the *Book of Offices* that predate and supplement Weyer via Scot. Meanwhile, by far the greatest similarity of *Offices* with Weyer is to be found between the 1st column and Weyer's 1st 18. By contrast there is very noticeably less convergence between the list of spirits who are ruled by Egin as given here and those of all the other catalogues. This is one among various indications in the literature of longstanding textual problems concerning Northern spirits. While ranks are omitted in this second part, cross referencing shows only one apparent Earl; otherwise these are Kings, Presidents, Dukes and Marquises. This suggests that Saleos aka Caleos once bore another rank besides Count or Earl. It may explain why each of the directional registers are 12 spirits long rather than 18 or more.

King	Oriens – East	Amaymon – South	Paymon – West	Egin – North
Deputy (sub king etc)	Baall/Bael	Asmoday	Beliall	Ozia
	Agaros (Agares)	Byleth	Barson (Balam, Abelam). Possibly identical with Baron etc.	Uriell/Uriall (Zagan. rpt)
	Barbas/Carbas (Marbas)	Astaroth	Gordosar	Usagoo (Vassago)
	Star (Shax)	Abech	Batath	Synoryell
	Semp (Vepar)	Berith	Mistalas (Stolas)	Tessan
	Algor (Eligor/Abigor)	Mallapar (Malphas)	Lechor (Allocer)	Goyle
	Seson (Pursan/Curson)	Partas (Foras, Parcas)	Saygayne, Laygayne (Zagan)	Auras
	Maxayn (Bathin/Machin)	Busin	Caleos (Saleos)	Othey
	Neophon (Glasyabolas etc)	Oze (Ose)	Cagyne, Cogin (Gamygyn)	Saranyt
	Barbas (Barbatos)	Pathyn (Haborym)	Suchay (Sucax of *clm 849*)	Muryell
	Amon (Aamon etc)	Cambra (Decarabia)	Reyall (Vual)	Umbra
	Suffales (Pruslas)	Gamor (Amy)	Layme (Cain and Raum)	Annaboth (Forcas. rpt)

Bealphares appears in a note below the 12 Northern names. Depending on your perspective, he may either belong or have subsequently been added to the system, appearing subsequently in the 'Presidential Council'. Similar names appear among lists of kings and messengers for the Four Kings in Hockley's *Offices* and elsewhere.

THE GERMAN *HONORIUS*

THE GERMAN FORM of *The Grimoire of Pope Honorius* originates in the C19th, despite which late date it deserves some attention (*CGP*). Among its contents are additional lists of spirits not found in earlier French and Italian versions, and one list in particular is extremely interesting.

German *Honorius*	Description, powers, things taught	Aliases elsewhere
Naema (suggests Nahema, Naamah)	Crowned woman on tall horse; teaches secret knowledge and heals sicknesses. Her kingdom is in the West.	Paimon.
Agarus	Old man teaches languages, gives power and might	Agares
St. Petrus [sic]	information, shows treasures, brings gold, silver etc	
Soas	Prince, reveals treasure, true answers	
Gamoet	King, reveals treasure	
Ampheron	Old man, treasure	
Neront	Bird, teaches and heals sickness, stirs quarrels, makes fools dance	
Siviant	True answers, strengthens the spirits and ensures they answer fully	Possibly Saranyt, (*Book of Oberon etc*)
Nemon	Upper half human, bearded, invoke for true answers, for powers of memory	
Baal	Great eastern King, invisibility, love	Baal (from here to Abigor are all in Weyer's 1st 18 etc)
Agerol	Old man, languages, lordship, wealth; teaches secret things and astrology	Agares (duplicated)

Heneral	Heals sickness, gives knowledge of healing and poisonous herbs	Buer (GoS etc) Gemer (LdE) Heramael (GV)
Johann? (? in MS)	Makes you loved, opens prisons	Gusoin/Gazon (GoS etc)
Artis	With two crowns and a sword, bestows favour	Artis/Botis Otis (GoS/LdE)
Machin	Powers of stones, plants, fetches same	Machin/Bathin or Mathim Trimasael (GV)
Jilbagor	Favour of princes	Abigor/Eligor (GoS etc)
Sibos	As an angel, makes wise and brave	
Gebepl	Language of birds, invisibility, catches thieves and murderers	
Zomal	Appears as water, makes rain	
Canfft	Bestows horses for the time needed	
Margolas	Makes quarrels, carries off castles and cities to other places (very garbled)	Malphas (GoS etc) Malpharas (LdE)
Sargas	Teaches powers of plants and stones, bestows health, wealth, invisibility	Forcas (Weyer etc) Parcas (LdE) Surgat (GV. GH)
Gezery	Bestows good workers, catches murderers	Gorsay, Gorsin (LdE)
Gewar	As a maiden, teaches all sciences, can transform herself into a bird if you wish	

Among the points of interest is the reference to Paimon as Naema, a name strikingly similar to Nahema. This is highly suggestive, Nahema being an important female figure from Jewish demonology and the myth cycles of some of the major spirits herein. Much of the background implicit here was covered extensively in TCM.

Seviant is possibly to be identified with Saranyt of the Book of Offices; the latter is a necromantic spirit and this may be what Seviant's power is referring to. Saranyt is crying out for further investigation for a variety of reasons.

The identification of Baal here is effortless, and several names subsequent to his are clearly from Weyer's first 18. The forms of their names are of great interest. In particular the rendering of Buer as Heneral clearly relates to the spelling used in the *Grimorium Verum*. Indeed, it was this entry in the German *Honorius* which led directly to the identification of Buer with Heramael in these researches. So too, once alerted by this instance, Trimasael's identity with Mathin/Machin arose, and the presence of Surgat under various names across a swathe of grimoires was detected. Once again, the importance of late period Continental grimoires in working back through our sources is deserving of emphasis.

Comparisons: Part One

First 18 spirits from Weyer

Weyer's spirits	Livre des Esperitz (list)	Livre des Esperitz (catalog)	Book of Offices (2 catalogs)	German Honorius and others
Bael	Veal	Beal	Bael, Baall	Baal
Agares	Agarat	Agarat	Acharos or Ahuras. Agaros.	Agarus, Agerol, (duplicates)
Marbas, Barbas	Barbas (prince)	Barthas	Corbas	
Pruslas, Busas	Bulfas (prince)	Bulfas	Suffales	Not in Scot or Goetia, but in Grand Grimoire, Offices/ Oberon and Livre des Esperitz
Amon, Aamon	Amon	Amon	Amon	
Barbatos	Batal (count)	Barbas (prince)	Barbates, Barbarys. Barbais.	clm 849 Barbarus
Buer	Gemen (king)	Gemer		Heneral (GV's Heramael etc)
Gusoyn	Gazon	Gazon		'Johann' clm 849 Cason
Botis, Otis	Artis (prince)	Artis	Oyga	Artis clm 849 Otius
Bathym (Bathin), Mathim	Machin	Machin	Marshioness, Maxayn	Machin (GV's Trimasael etc)
Pursan (Purson) Curson	Dicision	Diusion	Terson, Garsan, Gorsyar, Corsone, Seson.	clm 849 Curson

		FIRST 18 SPIRITS FROM WEYER CONTINUED		
Weyer's spirits	Livre des Esperitz (list)	Livre des Esperitz (catalog)	Book of Offices (2 catalogs)	German Honorius and others
Eligor, Abigor	Abugor	Abugor	Allogar, Algor,	Jilbagor clm 849 Alugor
Loray, Oray				
Valefar, Malephar				
Morax, Foraii			Formecones. Goorox	
Ipos, Ayperos	Vipos (count)	Vipos		
Naberus, (Naberius), Cerberus	Cerbere	Cerbere		Probably Nebiros, Nebirots etc In GV, GG, GH.
Glassy-Labolas, Caacrinolas, Caasimolar	Carmola (prince)	Carmola	Gloolas, Neophon	

The above table summarises the identities existing or likely between spirits in Weyer's first 18 and several other grimoires, including important spirit catalogues. Although several catalogues have been introduced at this point, examination of Weyer's text so far has been limited to the 1st 18 spirits. Before going further, it is necessary to introduce an important group. This is the Long Text group, of which there are five within Weyer's text; it is necessary to introduce them now because all five of them occur in the 2nd 18.

The Long Text Group

In the Weyer spirit catalogue few entries go beyond a few lines, with five major exceptions, which I imaginatively refer to as the 'Long Text group'. Of these five, one, Paimon, is the odd one out; Paimon belongs to the account of the upper hierarchy, otherwise omitted either by Weyer, or by his source. How this spirit came to be included is unknown, though a not unlikely explanation is existing duplication in the original, as paralleled elsewhere. Another is Weyer obscuring practical details. He does confess to deliberate tampering, and while the extent is unknown, evidence is mounting. In any case, the remaining four are Bileth, Belial, Asmoday, and Gaap. The interest of this group in understanding the text concerned is patent:

> These are the 72 Mighty Kings and Princes which King Solomon commanded into a vessel of brass, together with their Legions. Of whom Belial, Bileth, Asmoday, and Gaap, were Chief.
>
> *The Goetia of Solomon the King*

Many interesting details and hints about the relations of spirits with one another appear in these longer texts, which deserve closer examination in various reconstructive efforts. It is extremely likely that in a source previous to Weyer these Long Texts came before the main spirit catalogue, most likely accompanied by passages of similar scope detailing the Chiefs and other dignitaries.

As regards Long Texts, their origins and purpose, in my opinion they relate to exalted rank within the hierarchy, visible or invisible. The *Book of Offices* has significantly longer texts for the three Chiefs and the Four Kings; Falcas aka Lewteffar also receives a significantly longer entry. The *Livre des Esperitz* is generally brief, but gives the counterpart of Falcas more space than any. The most important for purposes of analysis is undoubtedly Weyer's group; these comparisons underline their importance. One major point of significance is that these specific Long Text entries are unique to Weyer/Scot. They are an important clue that these spirits have special significance in the overall hierarchy, supported by the presence of two of them at the top of *Offices'* directional columns.

I present first the Long Text entries in the English of Scot's *Discoverie of Witchcraft*. I have italicised various interesting or puzzling parts of the text.

THE LONG TEXTS

Bileth, is a great King and a terrible, riding on a pale Horse, before whom go Trumpets, and all kind of melodious Musick. When he is called up by an Exorcist, he appeareth rough and furious, to deceive him. Then let the Exorcist or Conjuror take heed to himself, and to allay his courage, *let him hold a hazel bat in his hand, wherewithal he must reach out toward the East and South, and make a triangle without besides the Circle*; but if he hold not out his hand unto him, and he bid him come in, and he still refuse the bond or chain of Spirits, let the Conjuror proceed to reading, and by and by he will submit himself, and come in, and do whatsoever the Exorcist commandeth him, and he shall be safe. If Bileth the King be more stubborn, and refuse to enter into the Circle at the first call, and the Conjuror shew himself fearful, or if he have not the chain of Spirits, certainly he will never fear nor regard him after: Also if the place be unapt for a triangle to be made without the Circle, then set there a boll of Wine, and the Exorcist shall certainly know when he cometh out of his house, with his fellows, and that the aforesaid Bileth will be his helper, his friend, and obedient unto him when he cometh forth. And when he cometh, let the Exorcist receive him courteously, *and glorifie him in his pride, and therefore he shall adore him as other Kings do, because he saith nothing without other Princes.* Also, if he be cited by an Exorcist, always a silver Ring of the middle finger of the left hand must be held against the Exorcists face, as they do for *Amaimon*. And the dominion and power of so great a Prince, is not to be pretermitted; *for there is none under the power and dominion of the Conjuror, but he that detaineth both men and women in doting love, till the Exorcist hath had his pleasure.*

He is of the orders of Powers, hoping to return to the seventh Throne, which is not altogether credible; and he ruleth Eighty five Legions.

Paimon, is more obedient to **Lucifer** than any other Kings are. Lucifer is here to be understood, he that was drowned in the depth of his knowledge: he would needs be like God, and for his arrogancy was thrown out into destruction, of whom it is said, 'Every pretious stone is thy covering'. Paimon is constrained by divine virtue to stand before the Exorcist, where he putteth on the likeness of a man: he sitteth on a beast called a Dromedary, which is a swift runner, and weareth a glorious crown, and hath an effeminate countenance: there goeth before him an host of men with Trumpets and well sounding Cymbals, and all Musical Instruments. At the first he appeareth with a great cry and roaring, as in Circulo Solomonis and in the Art is declared. And if this Paimon speak sometimes that the Conjuror understand him not, let him not therefore be dismayed. But when he hath delivered him the first obligation, to observe his desire, he must bid him also answer him distinctly and plainly to the questions he shall ask you, of all Philosophy, Wisdome, and Science, and of all other secret things. And if you will know the disposition of the World, and what the earth is, or what holdeth it up in the water, or any other thing, or what is Abyssus, or where the wind is, or from whence it cometh, he will teach you abundantly. *Consecrations* also, as well as Sacrifices, as otherwise may be reckoned. He giveth dignities and confirmations; he bindeth them that resist him in his own chains, and subjecteth them to the Conjuror; he prepareth good familiars, and hath the understanding of all Arts. *Note, that at the calling up of him, the Exorcist must look toward the Northwest, because there is his house.* When he is called up, let the Exorcist receive him constantly without fear, let him ask what questions or demands he list, and no doubt he shall obtain the same of him. And the Exorcist must beware he forget not the Creator, for those things that have been rehearsed before of Paimon; some say, he is of the order of

Dominions; others say, of the order of Cherubims. There follow him Two hundred Legions, partly of the order of Angels, and partly of Potestates. Note, that if Paimon be cited alone by an offering or sacrifice, *two Kings follow him; to wit, Bebal* [Belial], *and Abalam* [Balam, Barsan etc], *and other Potentates*; in his host are Twenty five Legions, because the Spirits subject to them are not alwayes with them, except they be compelled to appear by divine vertue.

Some say that the **King Belial** was created immediately after **Lucifer**, and therefore they think, that he was father and seducer of them which fell being of the orders: For he fell first among the worthier and wiser sort, which went before Michael, and other heavenly Angels, which were lacking. Although Belial went before all them that were thrown down to the earth, yet he went not before them that tarryed in heaven. This Belial is constrained by Divine virtue, when he taketh Sacrifices, Gifts, and Offerings, that he again may give unto the Offerers true answers. But he tarryeth not one hour in the truth, except he be constrained by the Divine power, as is said. He taketh the form of a beautiful Angel, sitting in a fiery Chariot; he speaketh fair, he distributeth preferments of Senatorship, and the favour of friends, and excellent familiars: He hath rule over Eighty Legions, partly of the order of Virtues, partly of Angels; he is found in the form of an Exorcist in the bonds of Spirits. The Exorcist must consider, that this Belial doth in every thing assist his subjects. If he will not submit himself, let the bond of Spirits be read: the Spirits chain is sent for him, wherewith wise Solomon gathered them together with their Legions in a brasen vessel, where were inclosed among all the Legions Seventy two Kings, *of whom the chief was* **Bileth**, *the second was* **Belial**, *the third* **Asmoday,** [GoS adds *and* **Gaap**] and above a thousand thousand Legions. Without doubt (I must confess) I learned this of my master Solomon; but he told me not why he gathered them together, and shut them up so; but I believe it was for the pride of this Belial. Certain Negromancers do say, that Solomon being on a certain day seduced by the craft of a certain Woman, inclined himself to pray before the same idol, Belial by name; which is not credible. And therefore we must rather think (as it is said) that they were gathered together in that great brasen vessel for pride and arrogancy, and thrown into a deep lake or hole in Babylon; for wise Solomon did accomplish his works by the Divine power, which never forsook him. And therefore we must think he worshipped not the image of Belial; for then he could not have constrained the Spirits by Divine virtue: *for this Belial, with three Kings*, were in the lake. But the Babylonians wondering at the matter, supposed that they should find therein a great quantity of treasure, and therefore with one consent went down into the lake, and uncovered and brake the vessel, out of the which immediately flew the Captain Devils, and were delivered to their former and proper places. But this Belial entered into a certain image, and there gave answer to them that offered and sacrificed unto him, as Tocz, in his sentences reporteth, and the Babylonians did worship and sacrifice thereunto.

Sidonay, aliàs **Asmoday**, a great King, strong and mighty, he is seen with three heads, whereof the first is like a Bull, the second like a man, the third like a Ram, he hath a Serpents tail; he belcheth flames out of his mouth; he hath feet like a Goose; he sitteth on an infernal Dragon, be carryeth a launce and a flag in his hand, he goeth before others which are under the power of Amaymon. When the Conjuror exerciseth this office, let him be abroad, let him be wary and standing on his feet; if his cap be on his head, he will cause all his doings to be bewrayed, which if he do not, the Exorcist shall be deceived by Amaymon in every thing. But so soon as he seeth him in the form aforesaid, he shall call him by his name, saying, Thou art Asmoday; he will not deny it, and by and by he boweth down to the ground; he giveth the ring of virtues, he absolutely teacheth Geometry, Arithmetick, Astronomy, and handicrafts. To all demands he answereth fully and truly; he maketh a man invisible; he sheweth the places where treasure lyeth, and gardeth it, if it be among the Legions of Amaymon; he hath under his power Seventy two Legions.

The last of the five requires so much examination that marking parts of it as 'interesting' with italics is pointless.

> **Gaap**, aliàs Tap, a great President and a Prince, he appeareth in a meridional sign [sic, and see Buer], and when he taketh humane shape, he is the guide of the four principal Kings, as mighty as **Bileth**. There were certain Necromancers that offered sacrifices and burnt offerings unto him; and to call him up, they exercised an art, saying, that Solomon the wise made it, which is false: for it was rather Cham, the son of Noah, who after the flood began first to invocate wicked Spirits. He invocated Bileth, and made an Art in his name, and a book which is known to many Mathematitians. There were burnt offerings and sacrifices made, and gifts given, and much wickedness wrought by the Exorcist, who mingleth therewithal the holy Names of God, the which in that Art are everywhere expressed. Marry there is an Epistle of those names written by Solomon, as also write Helias Aierosolymitanus and Helisaeus. It is to be noted, that if any Exorcist have the Art of Bileth, and cannot make him stand before him, nor see him, I may not bewray how, and declare the means to contain him, because it is an abomination, and for that I have learned nothing from Solomon of his dignity and office. But yet I will not hide this, to wit, that he maketh a man wonderful in Philosophy and all the Liberal Sciences; he maketh love, hatred, insensibility, and consecration of those things that are belonging unto the domination of **Amaymon**, and delivereth familiars out of the possession of other Conjurors, answering truly and perfectly of things present, past, and to come; and transferreth men most speedily into other Nations; he ruleth Sixty six Legions, and was of the order of Potestates.

GHOSTS IN THE MACHINE

THE ABOVE THEN are the five Long Text spirits (LT). Another important group of spirits in the catalogues is those with 'ghosts'. Ghosts are spirits in the same catalogue with similar to identical attributes and appearance to another spirit; a form of apparent redundancy worthy of closer examination.

MAJOR SPIRITS AND THEIR GHOSTS

Rank and Name			Form	Ghost
Paimon, King	LT		Rides a camel (accompanied by music)	Gomory: *GoS*, Duke Samon: *LdE*, King
Gaap President, King implied	LT	Guide	'In a meridional sign'(?) or in the form of a meridional spirit; human	Duplicated in *LdE*, much emphasised but problematic in *GoS*
Zagan King			Like a bull with griffons wings, human	Haagenti: *GoS*. President
Foras aka Forcas President in GoS, Prince in LdE			As a knight, with a pale horse, strong or cruel man, etc, double crown in some texts may indicate horns.	Furcas knight (sic) in *GoS*, duplicated as prince again in *LdE*. Several duplicates in *Offices*, all either Presidents or Governor, likely identical.

The above list is not intended to be exhaustive, but to illustrate that spirits with 'ghosts' often belong to important categories.

The Long Text group then consists of Bileth, Paimon, Belial, Asmoday, and Gaap, in that order. These spirits require a separate introduction before returning to the catalogue listings as with Weyer's 1st 18.

As regards the Long Text of Bileth's entry in the catalogue, much of this can be deferred for commentary later. Some comment is necessary in advance however, as the correspondingly long entry for Gaap consists almost entirely of a long 'digression' about Bileth. The most likely reading is that little besides the first line actually refers to Gaap at all; it has in fact been switched from an entry or entries concerning Bileth. Nor is this all; comparison of Gaap's entry in other catalogues shows that a smaller 'switch' has occurred in Bileth's Long Text. The powers with which he is credited are in fact Gaap's; those in Gaap's entry are part of Bileth's. This switching may be corruption and miscopying; another possibility is malicious tampering (for instance by Weyer to prevent the material being 'misused').

Paimon's entry needs, firstly, to be understood as belonging to an otherwise omitted earlier part of an original text similar to *Offices*. That is, following Lucifer, Belzebuth, and Satan's 'Long Texts', and accompanied by those of Oriens, Amaymon, and Egin. Ahead of an overdue new Latin translation, the direction to which Paimon is attributed here is problematic. 'Aquilonem' is here translated as North-West, however, scholars are only familiar with it and its adjectives meaning North, North-east and Northern, with North being the most common. None of these directions are associated with Paymon elsewhere, for whom, practically speaking, the most appropriate direction is the West anyway. An accurate spirit compass is thus impossible to derive from the Weyer text, particularly without recourse to decent Latinists, which I am not. The reference to two kings, Belial and 'Abelam', indicates the two spirits at the top of Paymon's column in *Offices*; Belial and Barson aka Balam, two kings mediating her power in the West.

Belial's text is, I think, relatively straightforward with one main exception:

> wise Solomon gathered them together with their Legions in a brasen vessel, where were inclosed among all the Legions Seventy two Kings, *of whom the chief was Bileth, the second was Belial, the third Asmoday. . .*
>
> Scot

To which the *Goetia of Solomon* adds

and Gaap

All these spirits have Long Text entries of course, but the change here, while subtle, is not unproblematic. Also *The Goetia* moves the text to a completely different place, after the main catalogue, as a kind of climax. I am inclined to consider this part of an attempted reconstruction; the addition of Gaap is understandable given other mentions in the existing text. However, justifiable or not, it fails as a clarification of hierarchical details and their attributions.

Asmoday's text, the shortest of the five, is also full of issues. *Cum hujus official exercet exorcista* should be 'when the exorcist would make use of the offices (incantations) of this [spirit]'. 'Let him be abroad' should be 'let him be strong'. The mention of a hat is not in the Latin, and in the English is perhaps derived from an old figure of speech; the Latin is all about overcoming fear, not how to dress.

Beyond the issues of poor translation, Gaap's text is far and away the most difficult and outright problematic. Almost all of it isn't about him at all but Bileth. The Goetia assumes the powers mentioned under both are correctly attributed; this is wholly unlikely. Gaap's powers as described in other, earlier, texts have very obviously been switched into Bileth's entry. Meanwhile Bileth, an enormously important but under-emphasised figure, has Gaap's, which are utterly trivial by comparison. Switching them back tells us an enormous amount about Bileth and gives us a much firmer grasp on the hierarchy.

COMPARISONS: PART TWO

WEYER'S SECOND 18. (1) = *LIVRE DES ESPERITZ*

Weyer	Rank Given	*Livre des Esperitz* (list)	*Livre des Esperitz* (catalog)
Zepar	Duke		
Bileth	King		
Sitri, Bitru	Prince	Bitur	
Paimon	King		
Belial	King	Brial	Vaal
Bune	Duke		Bune
Forneus	Marquis		
Ronove	Marquis, earl		
Berith+Beall, +Bolfry	Duke	Beal	Berteth
Astaroth	Duke	Estor	
Foras, Forcas	President	Parcas, (prince) Forcas (prince)	Parcas (prince)*
Furfur	Earl	Furfur (count)	Furfur
Marchosias	Marquis	Margotias	
Malphas	President		Malpharas
Vepar, Separ	Duke		
Sabnacke, Salmac	Marquis		Salmatis
Sidonay, Asmoday	King	Asmoday	Asmoday
Gaap, Tap	President and prince	Coap	Caap**

*this spirit has duplicate entries in LdE, Weyer/GoS.
** Prince Taob in *clm 849*

WEYER'S SECOND 18. (2) = BOOK OF OFFICES, GERMAN HONORIUS, AND OTHERS

Weyer's Spirits	Book of Offices List one	Book of Offices List two	German *Honorius* and others
Zepar	Hooab	Semp	
Bileth	Unidentified	Byleth	
Sitri, Bitru			GV Sergutthy etc
Paimon (King of the West	Paymon	Paymon	Probably Naema. + Raimond in the Conjurations. Gaeoneron in *clm 849* has affinities with both Paimon and Gomory.
Belial	Belial	Belial	
Bune			
Forneus			
Ronove			
Berith+Beall, +Bolfry	Berith	Berith	
Astaroth		Astaroth	Elestor* etc
Foras, Forcas	Annobath. Also Lewteffar aka Falcas (much elaborated)	Annoboth, Anoboth	German *GH* Sargas GV and *GH* Surgat
Furfur			
Marchosias			
Malphas		Mallapar	Margolas
Vepar, Separ			
Sabnacke, Salmac			
Sidonay, Asmoday		Asmoday	
Gaap, Tap			*clm 849* Taob

Lansdowne 1202 and *Wellcome 4669* MSS

ZEPAR...

Weyer's spirits	Book of Offices 1st list	Book of Offices 2nd list	Others
Zepar	Possibly Hooab	Unidentified	Possibly Sephar, Sunday demon *Hygromanteia*

ZEPAR, MATHERS' GOETIA

Zepar is a great duke, appearing as a souldier, inflaming women with the loove of men, and when he is bidden he changeth their shape, untill they maie enjoie their beloved, he also maketh them barren, and six and twentie legions are at his obeie and commandement.

Scot

There are no indications of a connection to Vepar, despite a similarity of names. On the other hand, while inconclusive, his powers are very similar to descriptions of Gaap (aka Taob in *LdE*), and Hooab could equally represent a form of that name. The possibilities inherent in a ducal form of Gaap are worth entertaining.

BILETH...

Weyer's spirits	Livre des Esperitz (list)	Livre des Esperitz (catalog)	Book of Offices 2nd catalogue	Others
Bileth	Unidentified	Byleth	Byleth	Found in *Juratus*, *Heptameron*, *clm 849*, and many others

BELETH, MATHERS' *GOETIA*

BILET, *PLUT.* 89

One of the most intriguing figures in the grimoires, Bileth deserves a lot more attention from researchers and practitioners alike. He – or possibly she – is named in three out of the five Long Text entries in the Weyer/Scot catalogue, and is plainly an important spirit.

Another translation of Scot's opening lines: 'Byleth, a great and terrifying king riding a fallow horse, headed by trumpets, orchestra and many other kinds of musicians'. A fallow (literally pale) horse was a medieval symbol of deceit.

Widely present outside the main family of grimoires to which the *Goetia* belongs; the name and sigil of Bileth are found in *ms. Plut.*89

Sup.38 with other chiefs of the spirits. In Weyer Bileth is accompanied by a wealth of fascinating detail. For example, the origin of the Triangle of Art – beloved of modern magicians influenced by the *Goetia* – is found in Weyer's account of Bileth.

> When he is called up by an Exorcist, he [Bileth] appeareth rough and furious... ... let the Exorcist or Conjuror take heed to himself, and to allay his courage, *let him hold a hazel bat in his hand, wherewithal he must reach out toward the East and South, and make a triangle without besides the Circle.*
>
> Scot

Note that while the Kings are usually associated with one direction of the compass, the figure mentioned here is drawn between two of them. The reasons for this are non-apparent, and in Paimon's case 'North-West' is definitely faulty translation.

The protective Ring of Solomon that features in the *Goetia* is mentioned in regard to Bileth, with other more cryptic advice:

> And when he cometh, let the Exorcist receive him courteously, *and glorifie him in his pride, and therefore he shall adore him as other Kings do, because he saith nothing without other Princes.*
>
> Scot

While previous editors and compilers have doubtless mangled this passage, it is perhaps possible to make some sense of it. Plainly Bileth is a figure to be treated with some courtesy and respect; moreover – as a reasonable supposition – other superior spirits must be invoked, or even conjured and present, in order for Bileth to cooperate with the magician.

In the Long Text pertaining to Belial, still more detail concerning Bileth emerges:

> ...wise Solomon gathered them [the spirits]... ...in a brasen vessel, where were inclosed... Seventy two Kings, of whom the chief was Bileth, the second was Belial, the third Asmoday. . .
>
> Scot

This is where Weyer's list ends. The *GoS* - with some textual justification - adds:

and **Gaap.**

While a subtle and perhaps understandable addition, this adds some difficulties as the text stands. There are all manner of complications relating to various groups of Four Kings, and not all such groups are interchangeable. Here however the sense is plain enough; this group of three, or four, are among the spirits in the vessel and very prominent among them. They are clearly distinct from such a group as Oriens, Amaymon, Paimon, and Egyn who are exterior to the vessel and superior to those within it. Within this interior group however it is clear that Bileth holds a position of extraordinary importance.

Under Gaap, mentioned above, appears yet another reference to Bileth. It is said that when Gaap

> taketh humane shape, *he is the guide of the four principal Kings, as*
> *mighty as* **Bileth**
>
> Scot

The reference to 'four principal kings' likely refers to the exterior group, in which case the title 'guide' indicates the function of Bileth and the other three kings, the interior group intermediate between these and the other spirits. The practical importance of establishing this is apparent.

While this passage supposedly concerns Gaap, after this it breaks off into a lengthy digression about Bileth. Indeed, how much of the text actually concerns Gaap (on whom information is already relatively scant) is wide open to question. For our present purposes however it is invaluable:

> Cham, the son of Noah... ...invoked Bileth, and made an Art in
> his name, and a book which is known to many Mathematitians
> [ie, magicians].
>
> Scot

The full passage plainly disapproves of this Art, and some of the text may be Weyer's. Sacrifices, burned offerings and incantations are mentioned, and connections with wise Solomon rather than sinful Cham are disavowed, although the sources of this Art are undoubtedly authentic Solomonic magic. Indeed, we possess some vestige of this Art of Bileth at very least in *clm 849* (No.23. *FR.* 242). In this fascinating text is described 'the first mirror of Lilit' (or Lylet, i.e. Lilith). Partway through the text the spelling 'Lilit' changes to 'Bylet', thus raising a fascinating conjecture. Namely, that our Bileth, undoubtedly a very important spirit herein, was previously identical with the equally potent figure of Lilith. See also my *TCM* where Lilith is shown to be the foremost of four queens of spirits, paralleling the status here.

The ritual concerns a magical mirror consecrated to the spirit. It is called *primum speculum Lilith*, the first mirror of Lilith. This primary status is unlikely to imply other Lilith mirrors, although other mirrors are certainly implied. What is more likely is that it is first among such mirrors due to the status of the spirit concerned. It concerns her and also *suorum virorum*, which may be translated in various ways, and the subtleties are considerable. *Vir* indicates man or husband. *Virorum* could therefore mean the husbands of Lilith; or, alternatively 'men' (soldiers and so forth) under her authority. The passage continues *suorumque militum seniorum*, and the leaders of her knights or soldiers. *Militum* relates to 'miles'; the term in Weyer's Latin text that English forms of the text translate arbitrarily as knights or soldiers.

This passage may thus accidentally clarify what is intended by knights in the *Goetia* and elsewhere. For the seniors are apparently named in the incantation following, leaving the knights or soldiers merely implicit under them. For me at least this suggests that knights and soldiers in the catalogues may be understood as comprising the frequently mentioned legions.

Such operations we are told must be performed in this mirror (implying that others are not suitable perhaps). The names employed in the ritual, if I understand the wording correctly, must be committed to memory. Moreover, and this is a fascinating detail, the rite is 'best performed in a clean place before Cain' (*ante Caym* in the Latin). To say the least, such a blasphemous instruction is not common in ceremonial magic, any more than the name Lilith is, at least apparently. However, Bileth is another matter; the name is ubiquitous in grimoire literature, as will briefly be shown.

In the *Book of Offices* Byleth is listed first after Amaymon, and a Southern correspondence for Lilith is also traditional. However, in the early and influential *Heptameron,* Bilet appears as the first minister of King Arcan who rules Monday, whose direction is the West.

The *Sworn Book* or *Liber Juratus* is a yet more venerable source, or certainly a strong parallel, for the *Heptameron* material. There Bileth is listed separately in similar lists of lunar and additional Westerly spirits in the shorter manuscripts. More complete texts of the system give a fuller picture, where all the kings and ministers are invoked not separately but together in varying combinations. In other words, Bileth is an essential minister for all of these workings, not only on Monday, but on all days. While there is room for a degree of uncertainty, only four of thirty or so *Heptameron/Juratus* names can be identified in the Weyer and *Oberon* spirit lists, so Bileth's presence there is conspicuous.

The appearance of Bilet in *ms. Plut.89 Sup.38* has already been mentioned. So too Bileth or Byleth is found in the Presidential Council of the Great Kings in *Offices, Oberon* and elsewhere, implicitly or explicitly. In the second set of *Offices* tables Byleth and Asmoday are the foremost kings under Amaymon. This appears to raise difficulties in interpretation of the Long Text group, if two of the four serve the same greater king, but these are not beyond resolution. More importantly meanwhile, Bileth is clearly a persistent high status figure in the grimoire spirit tradition. These characteristics may derive from an older identity as Lilith, a true queen of hell.

SITRI...

Weyer's spirits	Livre des Esperitz list	Others
Sitri, Bitru	Bitur	GV Sergutthy

SITRI, MATHERS' GOETIA

Sitri, alias Bitru, is a great prince, appeering with the face of a leopard, and having wings as a griffen: when he taketh humane shape, he is verie beautiful, he inflameth a man with a womans love, and also stirreth up women to love men, being commanded he willinglie deteineth secrets of women, laughing at them and mocking them, to make them luxuriouslie naked, and there obeie him sixtie legions.

Scot

Sitri aka Bitru is known in the *Book of Spirits* (Bitur) but as far as can be told is not present in the *Book of Offices*. On the other hand, the GV includes a likely counterpart, Sergutthy, in association with Heramael (Buer) and Trimasael (Mathim) – see Additional Spirits (page 112). If the identification of Sitri with Sergutthy is correct, only Sustugriel in this group is so far unidentified.

PAIMON...

Weyer's spirits	Livre des Esperitz (list)	Livre des Esperitz (catalog)	Book of Offices (2 catalogs)	Others
Paimon (King of the West	Poymon	Poymon	Paimon	Probably Naema. + Raimond in the Conjurations (German *Honorius*). Gaeoneron in *clm 849* has affinities with both Paimon and Gomory.

PAYMON, FROM JACQUES COLLIN DE PLANCY'S *DICTIONNAIRE INFERNAL*

PAIMON, MATHERS' GOETIA

King of the West and Elemental Air, Paimon is a very important figure in the spirit catalogues, of which the *LdE* is among the more clear and concise.

> Poymon appears in the semblance of a crowned woman, very resplendent, and rides a camel. He who constrains him must have his face towards the west, and he says truth of that which one asks him about and teaches all sciences to the master, and manifests all hidden things, and gives dignities and great lordships, and brings malefactors to plead for the master's mercy openly; and is lord of 25 legions.
>
> Scot

The familiar *GoS* gives 'an effeminate countenance', based I feel on an ambiguous Latin original. The French text is far clearer, at least as regards appearance. The gender of Paimon is perhaps a controversial subject, but there is little doubt that the 'classic' appearance is female, whatever rationalisations have occurred since. A general masculinising of spirits in Latin-derived grimoires is likely, whether theological or linguistic. Peterson suggests this originates with Trithemius; it is not typical of earlier Greek and Jewish texts. The subject of Queens of the spirits is an enormous one, partially accomplished in my *TCM*. That the earlier Greek forms of the catalogues contained female spirits is beyond doubt.

Meanwhile the *LdE* begins by detailing its upper hierarchy; as the second of the four kings below the infernal triad, Paimon is its 5th spirit. The *Book of Offices* has a listing with a similar, more detailed format. These examples of clarity are welcome, for elsewhere in the literature matters are far more obscure. A more careful examination is necessary with other English and German materials; Scot, GoS and clm 849, Weyer, the German *Honorius* and so forth.

As mentioned previously, Paimon's entry in Weyer's text is one of the five 'Long Texts'. Paimon is also a major dignitary of another group, those with 'ghosts'.

The first of Paimon's ghosts appears in Weyer:

> Gomory a strong and a mightie duke, he appeareth like a faire woman, with a duchesse crownet about hir midle, riding on a camell, he answereth well and truelie of things present, past, and to come, and of treasure hid, and where it lieth: he procureth the love of women, especiallie of maids, and hath six and twentie legions.

Weyer's Paimon also *weareth a glorious crown*, and the position of Gomory's is likely an error. Back to Gomory however it is to be noted that she is a 'duke' (the duchess crown may be an editorial joke, and note 'hir middle'). Note, spirits of ducal rank can be found in the Presidential Council, a position which may explain 'ghosting' in the sources.

Paimon also has a ghost in *LdE*, with a not dissimilar name, the same title of rank, a strong likeness in appearance and other duplications.

> Samon is a great king who appears in the semblance of a beautiful virgin. He gives response to that which one asks him about. He teaches [of] the goods and the treasures which are hidden and perfectly grants the love of all queens and women, be they virgins are not; and has 25 legions.

There are two possibilities regarding kingly rank in this case. Firstly, the entire entry represents duplication of the entry for Paimon as one of the Four Kings; this would be simple, but still lacks sufficient explanation. Another possibility is that here 'king' represents the other kind of King, such as Baal, operating on another level. This interpretation follows the hypothesis that the ghosting in the catalogues represents a consistent pattern. Judging from internal evidence, duplications originally alluded to the tiered conjuration process and multiple levels on which specific spirits operate within it. Subsequent copying, re-shaping, omissions and abbreviations obscured the structure; this led to 'ghosts', appearing as separate entities rather than as multiple references. This still leaves room for 'paths' of the spirit, also subordinates like unto them and sent in their place.

Potentially then, Paimon may function as both kinds of king, as well as a duke. In any case the first listing of spirits in *Offices/Oberon* has a duke Gemyem, of female appearance, wearing a duchess crown, with camel etc. Very plainly a counterpart of Gomory and thus a Paimon ghost. So too we find therein Lord Carmeryn or Cayenam with very similar qualities. There is even a Captain Gemon, with significantly fewer legions, but identical appearance and other features. As mentioned under Oray, 'Captain' may be another term for Duke, a title already accorded Gomory.

As regards the names, clearly Gemyem and Gemon are similar enough to one another, and Cayenam is similar also. Similar too in both name and attributes is duke Gaeoneron in *clm 849*. Does this apparent muddle represent an original multi-levelled structure reduced to an undifferentiated listing? I believe so.

So too in the German *Honorius* is found the spirit Naema, *a crowned woman on a 'tall horse'; she teaches secret knowledge and heals sicknesses, her kingdom is in the West*. The name of this spirit strongly suggests Nahema aka Naamah, a demon queen of Jewish tradition. It appears indubitable that Naema is to be identified with Paimon, further connecting her with older traditions concerning demon queens (*TCM* passim).

BELIAL...

Weyer's spirits	Livre des Esperitz (list)	Livre des Esperitz (catalog)	Book of Offices (2 catalogs)	Others
Belial	Brial	Vaal	Belial	

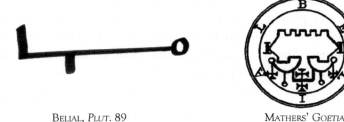

BELIAL, *PLUT.* 89   MATHERS' GOETIA

Belial is an important King, who appears in the Long Text group, both in his own entry and mentioned in Paimon's beside:

> ... two Kings follow him; to wit, Bebal [Belial], and Abalam [Balam, Barsan etc], and other Potentates.
>
> Scot

These identities may be checked with reference to the *Book of Offices*. Paimon has two sub-kings, Belial and Balaam, of whom Belial is premier. This is perhaps the clearest case in the entire hierarchy as regards which King is served by which deputies. Belial's attribution to the West in the relevant systems is thus clearly established.

The catalogue of Weyer, and the *Goetia* after him, includes an account of an image of Belial:

> the Babylonians... uncovered and brake the vessel, out of the which immediately flew the Captain Devils, and were delivered to their former and proper places. But this Belial entered into a certain image, and there gave answer to them that offered and

Pandemonium: A Discordant Concordance of Diverse Spirit Catalogues

sacrificed unto him, as Tocz, in his sentences reporteth, and the Babylonians did worship and sacrifice thereunto.

Scot

Claude Lecouteux mentions a ritual of image magic in a manuscript in Ghent, University Library (*ms. 1021 B, fol. 71*). The image is prepared when the Sun is setting and the Moon rising on the Day of Mercury. The feet, interestingly, are to face backwards, otherwise the image is of a man; the accompanying illustration has long hair. As the matter is of some interest, and extends to two similar images, I summarize the details here. Folk-ish and thoroughly Solomonic elements are both concurrent and apparent:

> The image is made from virgin wax and the ritual takes several days, including sprinkling with special water, smearing with the blood of a slain chicken and engraving with characters; further sprinklings, censings and an offering of coins; further days and the sacrifice of a pigeon, sprinkling the image again. After which the image is struck with a hazel wand and commanded, and will thereafter function as an oracle and will answer any questions you wish. The image is portable, and may be carried with you; it is to be kept hidden.

Comparisons with various instructions in the *Key of Solomon* are significant (*How to render oneself invisible*, (Mathers KoS I, x, from *Lansdowne 1203*; and KoS II, xviii).

BUNE...

Weyer's spirits	*Livre des Esperitz* catalog
Bune	Bune

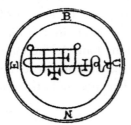 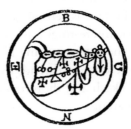

BUNE, MATHERS' *GOETIA*

Bune is a great and a strong Duke, he appeareth as a dragon with three heads, the third whereof is like to a man; he speaketh with a divine voice, he maketh the dead to change their place, and divels to assemble upon the sepulchers of the dead: he greatlie inricheth a man, and maketh him eloquent and wise, answering trulie to all demands, and thirtie legions obeie him.

Scot

By comparison with Bael and Balam, Bune's three heads point to an important place in the hierarchy which is so far not fully understood. His necromantic associations are particularly interesting; most of the contemporary grimoires tend to downplay the role of the dead, and only a select group of spirits have such connections. This may assist future identifications between such spirits.

FORNEUS...

Weyer's spirits	Others
Forneus	Unidentified

FORNEUS, MATHERS' *GOETIA*

Forneus is a great marquesse, like unto a monster of the sea, he maketh men woondeffull in rhetorike, he adorneth a man with a good name, and the knowledge of toongs, and maketh one beloved as well of foes as freends: there are under him nine and twentie legions, of the order partlie of thrones, and partlie of angels.

Scot

Forneus is sadly lacking in identifiable analogues, as are a good few of the Weyer/*Goetia* spirits. While those with several such analogues may be seen as important, some with few or no apparent analogues nevertheless deserve prioritising for future research. The sea monster is an interesting form, and conceivably links him with other aquatic forms in the catalogues.

RONOVE...

Weyer's spirits	Others
Ronove	Unidentified

RONWE, FROM JACQUES COLLIN DE PLANCY'S *DICTIONNAIRE INFERNAL*

Ronove a marquesse and an earle, he is resembled to a monster, he bringeth singular understanding in rhetorike, faithfull servants, knowledge of toongs, favour of freends and foes; and nineteene legions obeie him.

Scot

Ronove is another Weyer/*Goetia* spirit with few apparent analogues.

BERITH...

Weyer's spirits	Livre des Esperitz (list)	Livre des Esperitz (catalog)	Book of Offices (2 catalogs)	Others
Berith, Beall, Bolfry	Beal	Berteth	Berith	Berith, *Heptameron, clm 849, ms. Plut.89 Sup.38.* and numerous others

BERITH, *PLUT.* 89

MATHERS' GOETIA

The matter of this Duke's multiple names, and the different practitioners who employed them, has been dealt with elsewhere (see Appendix). Scot's text gives the essentials:

Berith is a great and a terrible duke, and hath three names. Of some he is called Beall; of the Jewes Berithi; of Nigromancers Bolfry: he commeth foorth as a red souldier, with red clothing, and upon a horsse of that colour, and a crowne on his head. He answereth trulie of things present, past, and to come. He is compelled at a certeine houre, through divine vertue, by a ring of art magicke. He is also a lier, he turneth all mettals into gold, he adorneth a man with dignities, and confirmeth them, he speaketh with a cleare and a subtill voice, and six and twentie legions are under him.

Scot

The ring mentioned is presumably the Ring of Solomon, and implies both bad breath and high rank. Given this, the text is likely more succinct than comprehensive. Possibly Weyer may even have taken scissors to it. One might be forgiven for being alert to possible aliases in the grimoire genre that will cast greater light on this particular spirit, particularly among names with a Bael or Baal prefix.

MS *clm 849* mentions this spirit repeatedly, and high status is frequently implied; for example, 'by your lords to whom you are bound in obedience – Sobedon, Badalam and Berith'. This passage occurs in a ritual naming Tubal as a demon, No.3 of the experiments in the text; Badelam is likely another spelling of Balaam. Experiment No.1 also conjures him as one of a trio in order to command other demons (with Apolin and Maraloth, the former present in *ms.Plut.82 Sup.38* and recension C of the *ToS*). Subsequently in this rite the same three are mentioned with other superiors, including Sathan, Beliath (sic), Belzebuc (sic) and Lucifer. Plainly then, Berith is a very high status spirit. In his commentary Keickhefer mentions a conjuration of Berith performed in Paris in 1323, in a circle of black cat's skin. In all these experiments incidentally, Berith's aid is sought in matters quite distinct from those in the catalogue, suggesting a far wider brief.

In the *Book of Offices* he is listed under the Southern jurisdiction of Amaymon. Also, as might be expected, Berith has a part in the Spirit Council.

ASTAROTH...

Weyer's spirits	Livre des Esperitz (list)	Livre des Esperitz (catalog)	Book of Offices (2 catalogs)	Others (selected for useful reference; the name's currency is ubiquitous)
Astaroth	Estor		Astaroth	Elestor, Elector in *Lansdowne 1202* Elestor in *Wellcome MS 4669* Astarot in *ms. Plut.89 Sup.38*

ASTAROTH, FROM JACQUES COLLIN DE PLANCY'S *DICTIONNAIRE INFERNAL*

ASTAROT, *PLUT.* 89

ASTAROTH, MATHERS' *GOETIA*

Astaroth is a great and a strong duke, comming foorth in the shape of a fowle angell, sitting upon an infernall dragon, and carrieng on his right hand a viper: he answereth trulie to matters present, past, and to come, and also of all secrets. He talketh willinglie of the creator of spirits, and of their fall, and how they sinned and fell: he saith he fell not of his owne accord. He maketh a man woonderfull learned in the liberall sciences, he ruleth fourtie legions. Let everie exorcist take heed, that he admit him not too neere him, bicause of his stinking breath. And therefore let the conjuror hold neere to his face a magicall ring, and that shall defend him.

Scot

Astaroth frequently appears as one of three or four ultimate superiors in spirit hierarchies as far back as the *Hygromanteia* and continuing into the C18th and on. My previous works (*TG*, *TCM*) have involved lengthy discussions of Astaroth, little of which requires recapitulation or revision. Briefly, the Old Testament name is part of the process of demonization rather than a real historical linkage (see particularly *TCM* on the *Testament of Solomon* and its context). The likeliest association with a pagan goddess is to Artemis Ephesia (Diana in Roman and New Testament sources), and thence – by established association – to Hecate.

This in turn likely explains his or her uniquely complex status across various spirit lists. A Duke according to the *Goetia*, but comparison with the *True*, *Grand* and *Honorian* grimoires suggests this is a special usage of the rank. Skinner goes so far as to suggest Kingly status, to account for such variants when employing the *Goetia*. Astaroth is a dignitary of the South according to the *Book of Offices*. South does have particular demonic associations with feminine spirits; perhaps it is best not to make overmuch of that here. Nonetheless, Hecate's general rulership of ghosts and other aerial spirits in Late Antiquity is important when considering how the same spirits provide the model – or biography – of the grimoire spirits in general. This likely explains why, when first encountering the LBA/LBS variants, she appears to 'compete' with Satan, who governs the Four Kings of these same aerial spirits. Interestingly, Astarot in *ms. Plut.89 Sup.38* is listed in a cluster including Belzebuth and the Four Kings (*Lec.* Ch.1.).

FOR⅃S...

Weyer's spirits	*Livre des Esperitz* (list)	*Livre des Esperitz* (catalog)	*Book of Offices* (2 catalogs)	Selected Others
Foras or Forcas	Parcas, (prince) Forcas (prince)	Parcas (prince)	Annobath, Annoboth, Anoboth. Also Lewteffar aka Falcas (much elaborated)	Surgat, GV *and GH* Surgat; Sargas in German *Honorius*

FORCAS, FROM JACQUES COLLIN DE PLANCY'S *DICTIONNAIRE INFERNAL*

SURGAT, FRENCH *VERUM*

FORAS, MATHERS' *GOETIA*

A variety of names, and textual errors in the *Goetia*, has obscured the importance of this spirit. He is undoubtedly one of the most important spirits integral to the conception(s) portrayed in the various catalogues. Although enlarged upon in recent times in *A Prince among Spirits*, that is recent enough to justify being fairly comprehensive here.

In Scot/Weyer/GoS the spirit has two entries; that is, he has a 'ghost', as distinguished from simple accidental duplication:

> Foras, aliàs Forcas, is a great President, and is seen in the form of a strong Man, and in humane shape, he understandeth the virtue of hearbs and pretious stones; he teacheth fully Logick, Ethicks, and their parts; he maketh a man Invisible, Witty, Eloquent, and to live long; he recovereth things lost, and discovereth treasures, and is Lord over Twenty nine Legions.
>
> Scot

> Furcas, is [appears as] a Knight, and cometh forth in the similitude of a cruel Man, with a long beard and a hoary head; he sitteth on a pale horse, carrying in his hand a sharp weapon; he perfectly teacheth practick Philosophy, Rhetorick, Logick, Astronomy, Chiromancy, Pyromancy, and their parts: there obey him Twenty Legions.
>
> Scot

As can be seen, the descriptions are not incompatible; a strong man is simply less detailed than a cruel one with beard and white hair. Teaching various subjects 'and their parts' is common to both. The *Livre des Esperitz* clarifies the matter of rank in the *Goetia*, where he is apparently the only knight. As duplicated therein he is a prince (president?) both times; there is no question of being a knight involved:

Parcas
Parcas is a great prince who makes a man subtle. He appears in a beautiful form. He knows the virtue of herbs and of precious stones and fetches them when commanded, and makes a man invisible and wise in all sciences, and makes a man become

young or old, as one desires, and restores the sight when one has lost it. And conveys gold and silver which is hidden in the earth and all other things, and carries the master throughout all the world if commanded, and all others if the master so commands; and he has beneath him xxx legions.

LdE

Forcas

Forcas is a great prince who teaches the virtue of herbs and precious stones, and makes one invisible and wise and well-spoken to all people, and will bring treasures concealed in the earth when commanded; and he has xxx legions.

LdE

The first of the *Book of Offices* catalogues describes him similarly:

Forcase, a great prince, appears like a great man (knight?); knows the virtue of all herbs and stones, restores lost sight, tells the places of treasures, gives true answers, and has 10 legions.

In the second listing he appears as Partas, under Amaymon; this is complicated by further considerations to be discussed below.

In the first listing again he makes, I believe, a second, much elaborated appearance. Here he bears an alias, Lewteffar as well as Falcas, Prince. He appears in monstrous form and speaks 'homely'; the speech of spirits is variously described in these grimoires, later it says he laughs and speaks hoarsely. He is mounted on a fiery dragon, and has 'starry eyes' and significantly, the head of a devil. His tail is a viper's, his hands of a bear, his feet of a mole. Also, 'he speaketh of great things' (possibly, 'with a great voice'?). His breast is open, his breath stinks, an apparent characteristic of particularly powerful spirits. He is crowned with a rainbow and his gaze is downward. He apparently loves music, which I think refers to musician attendants such as attend the Kings. The same passage tells us he appears in the 7th hour and has an eye in his forehead.

This wonderful portrait includes the same kind of specifics as others relating to the powers of Forcas elsewhere, again elaborated. Summarising the text: He heals sickness and disease; makes men seem mad, and rise up against another. He teaches the art of necromancy in five days. Knows 'every part of free love', and entices women to pride; making them love men.

The length and detail of the passage is only matched in Weyer's catalogue by Paimon, Asmoday, Gaap, Belial, and Bileth, all greater or lesser Kings. We are told he lies, and will not confess himself 'to be Abarak'. He will, moreover, claim to be one of the Four Kings. Regarding Abarak, Baraq in Hebrew means 'black' and in Arabic Al Baraq is 'thunder'. The Phoenician Barca, surname of famed generals, is related. This is similar to forms of this spirit's own name: Parcas/Falcas.

Thus the passage likely means he will pretend not to be himself but one of the Four Kings. This is an interesting aside, and underlines the status and power of the spirit. He desires sacrifice, I suspect in the same manner as with his various namesakes in *Honorius*, and is then a good informant. Also like the spirits of *Honorius*, he fetches treasure and money from one place to any place desired. So too he makes a man skilled in astronomy and astrology, geomancy and the liberal sciences. He gives promotions and dignities and has 20 legions. As Surgat, His appearance under the same name in the main *Verum* catalogue is significant. So far no other spirits therein have direct analogues in the *Goetia*, though others have been identified elsewhere in the grimoire.

Identifying the spirits of the grimoires with their analogues elsewhere is by no means an exact science. The status of this spirit has already been underlined. However, *Offices'* first listing also includes a strikingly similar spirit under a different name, who is earlier identified as one of the presidential counsellor spirits to the Four Kings. This is Annobath, here called a Lord and Governor, with the same meaning as President elsewhere. Although as Partas he already appeared as a Southern spirit, here he is listed under the spirits of the North. His appearance is as a knight on a pale horse, he wears a double crown which I suspect is elsewhere read as two horns, like Lewteffar with the head of a devil. He bears a spear in his hand. Like Forcas and the other aliases, he teaches necromancy, geomancy, and chiromancy, and the art magic. He tells who guards these secrets, and how they may be obtained. Like Falcas, he gives true answers. As a major spirit Annoboth/Anaboth also appears in the second listing. There too he appears as a knight who gives expertise in necromancy, shows where treasure is hidden and who guards it. If the guardian is a spirit of the North, he can drive them away. He can tell of 'wonderful strange things'.

That Partas appears in the column of Amaymon and Anaboth in that of Egyn is significant. A similar double placing occurs in relation to Seson and Gordosar; both are forms of King Pursan, placed in the column of Oriens and Paymon respectively. Also, Anaboth is named as one of the Presidential Council, as is Gordosar. This duplication, using different names or titles for two roles, is perhaps best interpreted both as structural and as adding depth to the picture of the spirit concerned.

Surgat appears also in the *Grimoire of Pope Honorius* (see below); he is indeed a key figure in the subtext of several grimoires.

For Sunday, to Surgat.

This experience is performed at night from eleven to one o'clock. He will demand a hair of your head, but give him one of a fox, and see that he takes it. His office is to discover and transport all treasures, and perform anything that you may will. Write in his circle: Tetragrammaton (x3). Ismael, Adonay, Ilma (or Ihua). And in a second circle: Come, Surgat! (x3).

Conjuration.

I conjure thee, O Surgat, by all the names which are written in this book, to present thyself here before me, promptly and without delay, being ready to obey me in all things, or failing this, to despatch me a Spirit with a stone which shall make me invisible to everyone whensoever I carry it! And I conjure thee to be submitted in thine own person, or in the person of him or of those whom thou shalt send me, to do and accomplish my will, and all that I shall command, without harm to me or to any one, so soon as I ake known my intent.

There are various significant features of relevance here. The connection with stones and invisibility is obviously a recurrent theme, of which more anon. In the meantime, the matter of aliases is considerably extended by the various forms of the *Honorius* text. In the *Honorius* text dated 1800 the spirit of Sunday is named as Aquiel, while the 1760 version calls him Surgat, in common with the Italian *Verum*. In the version dated 1670 he bears the name Acquiot. In all versions the same powers are described, and the ritual does not differ, strengthening the assumption that these are aliases rather than distinct spirits.

Aquiel appears in the *Heptameron* among the northern angels ruling the air on Sunday. However, he also strongly resembles Aciel and Aziel, associated with Sunday in some Faustian grimoires.

> Aciel: The mightiest among those who serve men. He manifests in pleasing human form about three feet high. He must be invoked three times before he will come forth into the circle prepared for him. He will furnish riches and will instantly fetch things from a great distance, according to the will of the magician. He is as swift as human thought.

This Faustian equivalence hints at connections beyond the *Heptameron* which supplied some of the conjurations in the *Honorius* grimoire, as it did in the *Goetia of Solomon*. A similar attribution of demons to days appears in the 6th and 7th *Books of Moses*. Nevertheless, while the spirit catalogues converge, detailed equivalences between the operating systems should not be assumed. Another point regarding Aquiel/Acial points to possible convergence with the geographical associations of *Verum* spirits. In the highly composite *Wellcome MS*, a spirit called Achel is mentioned separately as the spirit that 'rules and governs France'. This likely indicates a dovetailing of spirits of the week (including the three chiefs) with mundane rulership of continents and individual countries. France is traditionally ruled by Leo, the Sign of the Sun, suggesting that Achel and Aquiel the Sunday demon are at very least related.

From here the trail enters some very recondite areas. Aciel aka Azael or Asiel is a major figure of Jewish demonology, appearing in the *Book of Enoch* and elsewhere. As an angel name Azael or Asiel means 'whom God strengthens'. The *Zohar* mentions him in company with Aza as two fallen angels who cohabited with Naamah. This daughter of Lamech is herself prominent in traditional demonology, a Lamia figure also bearing the name Nahema. The Zoharic tradition gives the origin of the Sedim (satyr-like spirits) as occurring with this pairing. The *Midrash Petirat Mosheh* gives a related story where he descends from heaven with Ouza (compare Aza) and is corrupted. Agrippa and others list him among four evil angels of the elements. These spirits are distinct from the Four Kings (Oriens, Paymon, Amaymon, and Egyn), and are occasionally represented as their emanations. With such great dignity among the Fallen Angels – Azael has been identified with Shemhazai/Semyaza – it is not surprising if this distinction occasionally becomes tenuous. In all probability the reference in the *Book of Oberon* to him denying his identity and claiming to be one of the Kings derives from this circumstance.

FURFUR...

Weyer's spirits	*Livre des Esperitz* catalog
Furfur	Furfur

FURFUR, FROM JACQUES COLLIN DE PLANCY'S *DICTIONNAIRE INFERNAL*

FURFUR, MATHERS' *GOETIA*

Furfur is a great earle, appearing as an hart, with a firie taile, he lieth in everie thing, except he be brought up within a triangle; being bidden, he taketh angelicall forme, he speaketh with a hoarse voice, and willinglie maketh love betweene man and wife; he raiseth thunders and lightnings, and blasts. Where he is commanded, he answereth well, both of secret and also of divine things, and hath rule and dominion over six and twentie legions.

Scot

Furfur is found, with identical spelling, in the oldest form of the catalogue we have (*LdE*). The above reference to the triangle may be important, although not present in all grimoires by any means. The form in *LdE* is different, being that of an angel. Also the weather-making powers are absent.

MARCHOSIAS...

Weyer's spirits	Livre des Esperitz catalog
Marchosias	Margotias

MARCHOCIAS, FROM JACQUES COLLIN DE PLANCY'S *DICTIONNAIRE INFERNAL*

MARCHOSIAS, MATHERS' GOETIA

Marchosias is a great marquesse, he sheweth himselfe in the shape of a cruell shee woolfe, with a griphens wings, with a serpents taile, and spetting I cannot tell what out of his mouth. When he is in a mans shape, he is an excellent fighter, he answereth all questions trulie, he is faithfull in all the conjurors businesse, he was of the order of dominations, under him are thirtie legions: he hopeth after 1200 yeares to returne to the seventh throne, but he is deceived in that hope.

Scot

The *Livre des Esperitz* knows this spirit. He has several similar elements in his appearance to other spirits, who likely form some kind of group. The appearances of the spirits are almost certainly some kind of mnemonic code – see Frances Yates' works – which we no longer understand or even emphasise in research overmuch.

MALPHAS...

Weyer's spirits	Livre des Esperitz catalog	Book of Offices 2nd list	German Honorius
Malphas	Malpharas	Mallapar	Margolas

MALPHAS, FROM JACQUES COLLIN DE PLANCY'S *DICTIONNAIRE INFERNAL*

MALPHAS, MATHERS' *GOETIA*

Malphas is a great president, he is seene like a crowe, but being cloathed with humane image, speaketh with a hoarse voice, be buildeth houses and high towres wonderfullie, and quicklie bringeth artificers togither, he throweth downe also the enimies edifications, he helpeth to good familiars, he receiveth sacrifices willinglie, but he deceiveth all the sacrificers, there obeie him fourtie legions.

Scot

Birdlike spirits are another likely grouping within the system which is no longer understood. This President is among those readily identifiable in the Spirit Council, and thus an important figure within the overall hierarchy. The *Book of Offices* places him under Amaymon; he is also in Weyer's 2nd 18, with which Amaymon's *Offices* spirits overlap considerably.

VEPAR...

Weyer's spirits	Book of Offices list two
Vepar/Separ	Semp

VEPAR, MATHERS' *GOETIA*

Vepar, alias Separ, a great duke and a strong, he is like a mermaid, he is the guide of the waters, and of ships laden with armour; he bringeth to passe (at the commandement of his master) that the sea shall be rough and stormie, and shall appeare full of shippes; he killeth men in three daies, with putrifieng their wounds, and producing maggots into them; howbeit, they maie be all healed with diligence, he ruleth nine and twentie legions.

Scot

Despite a similar name to Zepar there are no indications of a connection between them. Semp or Semper is the *Offices/Oberon* form of Vepar. Obviously not in the first 18 of Weyer's spirits, so the Eastern placement is among the more speculative entries there.

SABNACKE...

Weyer's spirits	*Livre des Esperitz*
Sabnacke/Salmacke	Salmatis

SABNOCK, MATHERS' *GOETIA*

Sabnacke, alias Salmac, is a great marquesse and a strong, he commeth foorth as an armed soldier with a lions head, sitting on a pale horsse, he dooth marvelouslie change mans forme and favor, he buildeth high towres full of weapons, and also castels and cities; he inflicteth men thirtie daies with wounds both rotten and full of maggots, at the exorcists commandement, he provideth good familiars, and hath dominion over fiftie legions.

Scot

Lion's heads and pale horses are both visible attributes shared by various spirits and again likely indicate a code related to magical mnemonics and decan talismans.

ASMODAY...

Weyer's spirits	Livre des Esperitz (list)	Livre des Esperitz (catalog)	Book of Offices	Selected Others
Asmoday aka Sidonay	Asmoday	Asmoday	Asmoday	Asmodeus, *Testament* Asmodai, *Hygromanteia* Asmodee, *Abramelin.* etc

ASMODÈE, FROM JACQUES COLLIN DE PLANCY'S *DICTIONNAIRE INFERNAL*

ASMODAY. MATHERS' *GOETIA*

The inter-relations of Asmoday aka Asmodeus with other chiefs, as well as a major biography of this spirit, appeared in *TCM*. Suffice it to say that he is a major king with high status in various lists of spirits, going back to the *Hygromanteia*. He is also one of the four guides named in the *Goetia* (see Bileth, Belial, and Gaap) all having Long Text entries in Weyer/Scot. Asmoday is listed first under Amaymon, King of the South, in the *Book of Offices*. A difficulty here is that Byleth follows immediately after him, so that the four guides are unevenly shared among the kings. This apparent quandary decreases substantially once we assume not one kingly guide per direction but two, and make allowances for vagueness or confusion in the Weyer catalogue and its derivatives.

In the *Hygromanteia* tradition he is accounted one of the four major chiefs of demons, as discussed in *TCM*. He is also the demon of the Sun, countered by Michael, the chief of angels. This underlines him as a very significant figure, even more so given the standard solar emphasis.

GAAP...

Weyer's spirits	Livre des Esperitz (list)	Livre des Esperitz (catalog)	Book of Offices (2 catalogs)	Others
Gaap and Goap	Coap	Coap	Unidentified	clm 849 Taob

GAAP, MATHERS' GOETIA

The Long Text related to Gaap has been given previously, and comparisons with Bileth's were mentioned in the entry concerning the latter spirit. In the *Goetia* system at least he may be considered a 'guide' of the Four 'principall' Kings (Oriens, Amaymon, Paimon, and Egyn) as are Bileth, Beliall, and Asmoday. However, the Long Text form should be compared with that in *clm 849*:

> Taob is a great prince. He appears in the form of a doctor when he takes on a human form; is the best teacher/doctor of women and he makes them burn with love for men. If they are told he is [?], makes them to be transformed into another form, and those who have come before the beloved. The end makes them sterile. He hath under him 25 legions, etc.

And *LdE*:

> [23] Coap

Pandemonium: A Discordant Concordance of Diverse Spirit Catalogues

Coap is a great prince who gives use of women and brings them where one wants and makes them beside themselves if one commands him; he has 27 legions.

So that a reconstruction of Gaap's text in Weyer/Scot, assuming most of it pertains to Bileth, might well read like this:

> **Gaap**, aliàs Tap, a great President and a Prince, he appeareth in a meridional sign [sic?], and when he taketh humane shape, he detaineth both men and women in doting love, till the Exorcist hath had his pleasure. He is of the orders of Powers, hoping to return to the seventh Throne, which is not altogether credible; and he ruleth Eighty five Legions.

To swap or not to swap the angelic Order and number of legions between the two spirits remains arguable. Meanwhile, I suspect *clm 849*'s Latin (*signo medici*) is to be preferred to Weyer's, thus he has the form of a doctor rather than 'appearing in a meridional sign'.

To play devil's advocate (and why not in a directory of demons?), let us entertain the other reading. 'Meridional' might be explained in a variety of loosely related ways. Firstly, of course 'sign' likely implies 'shape or image' rather than a zodiacal Sign (still less a specific one). Thus in Agrippa we find:

> ...moreover they distinguish also this kind of Angels into Saturnine and Joviall, according to the names of the Stars, and the Heavens; further some are Orientall, some Occidentall, some Meridional, some Septentrionall. . .

Here the inference is directional; to be precise, southerly. So we might have 'of a southern appearance' as a legitimate reading. This is not as obscure as it may sound. The 'familiar forms of the spirits of Jupiter' (corresponding to the South wind in the *Heptameron*), are given in the *Fourth Book of Occult Philosophy*, in the chapter of the same name, to which the *Heptameron* refers directly. These include:

A King with a Sword drawn, riding on a Stag.
A Man wearing a Mitre in long rayment.
A Maid with a Laurel-Crown adorned with Flowers.

Also, for completeness' sake: a 'Bull, Stag, Peacock, azure Garment, Sword or Box-tree'.

However, another reading of meridional is possible, as explained by William Lilly:

> Some Signes are called Austral, Meridional or Southern, for that they decline Southward from the Equinoctial, and these are Libra, Scorpio, Sagittarius, Capricorn, Aquarius, Pisces.
>
> *Christian Astrology*

There is – of course – no reason whatever to prefer one of these 'Signes' above another, or to assume a connection with Gaap's shape from them.

Moreover, returning to Agrippa, yet another usage exists though probably conformable with the first given above:

> ...whence as these Angels are appointed for diverse Stars, so also for diverse places and times, not that they are limited by time or place, neither by the bodies which they are appointed to govern, but because the order of wisdom hath so decreed, therefore they favor more, and patronize those bodies, places, times, stars; so they have called some Diurnall, some Nocturnall, other Meridionall...

'Meridionall' here probably means midway between morning and evening, which is to say Noon, when the Sun is 'in the South', or, astrologically, 'in the tenth House'.

All in all, I consider correction via *clm 849* more straightforward' and justifying the oddness of the Weyer/*Goetia* text in isolation more convoluted and partial. Meanwhile, the mention of rule by Amaymon in Gaap's Long Text is problematic for various reasons. Firstly, it may refer to Gaap or to Bileth. Secondly, Amaymon is associated with the South in

Agrippa and elsewhere, but not in the *Goetia* as it currently stands. Bileth is certainly placed under Amaymon in *Offices*, a natural enough position for him. It is not certain the same rulership applies to Gaap, who is unidentified in that text at present. Indeed, we might reasonably expect one 'guide' per 'principall king' as an original standard here.

THE
SPIRIT CATALOGUES
PART THREE

COMPARISONS: PART THREE

WEYER'S THIRD 18. (1) = *LIVRE DES ESPERITZ*

Weyer's spirits	Rank	*Livre des Esperitz* (list)	*Livre des Esperitz* (catalog)
Chax (Shax), Scox	Marquis		Drap (duke)
Pucell (Procell)	Duke	Pucel	Bucal
Furcas	Knight		
Murmur	Duke, earl		
Caim	President		
Raum, Raim	Earl		
Halphas	Earl		
Focalor	Duke		
Vine	King, earl		
Bifrons	Unidentified		
Gamigin	Marquis		
Zagam (Zagan)	King, president	Zagon (and Dragon, Prince?)	Bugan (King)
Orias	Marquis		
Volac (Valac)	President		
Gomory	Duke		Samon (King, resembles Paymon)
Decarabia, Carabia	(not given)		
Amduscias	Duke		
Andras	Marquis		

WEYER'S THIRD 18. (2) = *BOOK OF OFFICES*, GERMAN *HONORIUS*, AND *OTHERS*

Weyer's Spirits	*Book of Offices* list one	*Book of Offices* list two	Others
Chax (Shax), Scox	Skor (duplicated)	Star	Possibly Skar (Saturday spirit, *Hygromanteia*)
Pucell (Procell)	Possibly Porax		
Furcas (duplicated)	Forcase. Possibly Gemmos and Asoryor, Antyor	Partas	
Murmur			
Caim			
Raum, Raim	Kayne	Layme	Zaym etc *Sloane* 3824
Halphas			
Focalor			
Vine			
Bifrons			
Gamigin	Sogan, Sogam	Cagyne, Cogin	
Zagam (Zagan)	Unidentified	Saygayne/Zagayne, Laygayne. also Uriell, Uriall (!)	
Orias			
Volac (Valac)	Coolor, Doolas		Volac *clm* 849
Gomory (resembles Paymon)	Gemyem. Carmeryn, Cayenam. Gemon.		Gaeneron German *Honorius*
Decarabia, Carabia	Possibly Barton, Bartyn	Cambria/Cambra	
Amduscias			
Andras			

SHAX...

Weyer's spirits	Livre des Esperitz list	Livre des Esperitz catalog	Book of Offices 1st list	Book of Offices 2nd list	Others
Shax, Scox	Deas	Drap	Skor (duplicated)	Star	Skar (Saturday spirit, *Hygromanteia*)

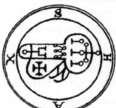

SHAX, MATHERS' GOETIA

Shax, alias Scox, is a darke and a great marquesse, like unto a storke, with a hoarse and subtill voice: he dooth marvellouslie take awaie the sight, hearing and understanding of anie man, at the commandement of the conjuror: he taketh awaie monie out of everie kings house, and carrieth it backe after 1200. yeares, if he be commanded, he is a horssestealer, he is thought to be faithfull in all commandements: and although he promise to be obedient to the conjuror in all things; yet is he not so, he is a lier, except he be brought into a triangle, and there he speaketh divinelie, and telleth of things which are hidden, and not kept of wicked spirits, he promiseth good familiars, which are accepted if they be not deceivers, he hath thirtie legions.

Scot

Sloane 3824 calls him Scor (or Scarus). The mention of a triangle is one of a few instances in Weyer's text (see Bileth and Furfur entries).

PROCELL, PUCEL...

Weyer's spirits	Livre des Esperitz list	Livre de Esperitz catalog	Book of Offices 1st list
Pucel	Pucell	Bucal	Possibly Porax

Procell is a great and a strong duke, appearing in the shape of an angell, but speaketh verie darklie of things hidden, he teacheth geometrie and all the liberall arts, he maketh great noises, and causeth the waters to rore, where are none, he warmeth waters, and distempereth bathes at certeine times, as the exorcist appointeth him, he was of the order of potestats, and hath fourtie eight legions under his power.

Scot

Weyer has Pucel, Scot's source has Procell; while not used in the GoS, LdE's Pucell is thus consistent with Weyer.

FURCAS...

Weyer's spirits	Book of Offices (2 catalogs)	Notes
Furcas (duplicate of Foras, Forcas in Weyer; thus also in Scot and the Goetia, where he is mistakenly ranked as knight.)	Forcase, Partas. Possibly Gemmos and Asoryor, Antyor.	Duplicated and greatly emphasised in accordance with actual rank in the *Book of Offices*.

FURCAS, MATHERS' GOETIA

Furcas is a knight and commeth foorth in the similitude of a cruell man, with a long beard and a hoarie head, he sitteth on a pale horsse, carrieng in his hand a sharpe weapon, he perfectlie teacheth practice philosophie, rhetorike, logike, astronomie, chiromancie, pyromancie, and their parts: there obeie him twentie legions.

Scot

See main entry under Foras, Forcas, page 165.

MURMUR...

Weyer's spirits	Others
Murmur	Unidentified

MURMUR, MATHERS' GOETIA

Murmur is a great duke and an earle, appearing in the shape of a souldier, riding on a griphen, with a dukes crowne on his head; there go before him two of his ministers, with great trumpets, he teacheth philosophie absolutelie, he constraineth soules to come before the exorcist, to answer what he shall ask them, he was of the order partlie of thrones, and partlie of angels, and ruleth thirtie legions.

Scot

While not found under this name in the other sources consulted, an appearance attended by ministers with trumpets suggests a spirit of great dignity. He should be identifiable elsewhere, perhaps even in the Spirit Council, probably under another name. He is one of the select few necromantic spirits, which also adds interest deserving of further research.

CAIM AND RAUM...

Weyer's spirits	Book of Offices 1st list	Book of Offices 2nd list	Others
Caim, Caym (Cain), Camio	Kayne	Layme or Zayme	Tame. *Sloane 3824*

CAYM, FROM JACQUES COLLIN DE PLANCY'S *DICTIONNAIRE INFERNAL*

CAMIO, MATHERS' *GOETIA*

Following Weyer's catalogue, rather than the *Goetia*, Caim and Raum are consecutive names. The paper trail strongly suggests Raum is a duplicate. Both spirits have a bird form; some sources give Caim the alternative of a black bird. Both have the same number of legions. Here are their entries from Scot:

> Caim is a great president, taking the forme of a thrush, but when he putteth on man's shape, he answereth in burning ashes, carrieng in his hand a most sharpe swoord, he maketh the best disputers, he giveth men the understanding of all birds, of the lowing of bullocks, and barking of dogs, and also of the sound and noise of waters, he answereth best of things to come, he was of the order of angels, and ruleth thirtie legions of divels.

> Raum, or Raim is a great earle, he is seene as a crowe, but when he putteth on humane shape, at the commandement of the exorcist, he stealeth woonderfullie out of the kings house, and carrieth it whether he is assigned, he destroieth cities, and hath great despite unto dignities, he knoweth things present, past, and to come, and reconcileth freends and foes, he was of the order of thrones, and governeth thirtie legions.

Offices, however, has a single spirit, Kayne, in its first list, who appears like a raven. He is a Duke concerned with thefts, carries treasures and gives favour of friends and enemies. In its second list he is Zayme (Peterson's reading) also a raven-formed carrier spirit, with the added detail of concern with buildings, cities, and castles, as well as dignities and honours. Thus far his powers suggest Raum or Raim, were it not for his presence on the Presidential Council, which really requires the dignity of Caym. In my opinion there was originally one spirit, Cain, crow or raven formed, with more than one rank. Caym also appears to be a (Gaelic and old French) form of Cain, a biblical name replete with demonological associations, at the same root level as Nahema/Paimon, Lilith/Bileth, and Parcas/Azael. A tantalising reference to Tubal in *clm* 849 No.3 may be connected (for arousing a woman's love). Cain is also mentioned in reference to a mirror of Lilith in *clm* 849 (see under Bileth, page 146).

HALPHAS...

Weyer's spirits	Others
Halphas	Unidentified

HALPHAS, MATHERS' *GOETIA*

Halphas is a great earle, and commeth abroad like a storke, with a hoarse voice, he notablie buildeth up townes full of munition and weapons, he sendeth men of warre to places appointed, and hath under him six and twentie legions.

Scot

Weyer and his derivatives appear to be the only sources for this spirit at present.

FOCALOR...

Weyer's spirits	Others
Focalor	Unidentified

FOCALOR, MATHERS' GOETIA

Focalor is a great duke comming foorth as a man, with wings like a griphen, he killeth men, and drowneth them in the waters, and overturneth ships of warre, commanding and ruling both winds and seas. And let the conjuror note, that if he bid him hurt no man, he willinglie consenteth thereto: he hopeth after 1000. yeares to returne to the seventh throne, but he is deceived, he hath three legions.

Scot

Three, imitated in the English MSS of the *Goetia* before Mathers corrected it, is an absurdly low number of legions for a duke; sure enough the Latin *Triginta* translates as 30. There is no apparent counterpart in *LdE* or *Offices*.

VINE...

Weyer's spirits	Book of Offices 1st list
Vine	Royne

VINE, MATHERS' GOETIA

Vine is a great king and an earle, he showeth himselfe as a lion, riding on a blacke horsse, and carrieth a viper in his hand, he gladlie buildeth large towres, he throweth downe stone walles, and maketh waters rough. At the commandement of the exorcist he answereth of things hidden, of witches, and of things present, past, and to come.

Scot

For a king Vine is at present little known, at least under that name. The description of Royne differs in some respects, but the identity is clear enough; I am more reticent of extending it to Morle or Goyle, despite some points of similarity. This is unfortunate, as that would give us a point of the compass with which to associate him.

More usefully however, the description in *Offices* gives a more elaborate account of his powers. Among these extra details, that 'he consecrates books and other things' has more the ring of an important king, once much consulted by magicians. How he faded compared to, say, Curson or Zagan, is impossible to say at this time. He is another spirit thoroughly deserving modern attention.

BIFRONS...

Weyer's spirits	Others
Bifrons	Unidentified

BIFRONS, MATHERS' GOETIA

Bifrons is seene in the similitude of a monster, when he taketh the image of a man, he maketh one woonderfull cunning in astrologie, absolutelie declaring the mansions of the planets, he dooth the like in geometrie, and other admesurements, he perfectlie understandeth the strength and vertue of hearbs, pretious stones, and woods, he changeth dead bodies from place to place, he seemeth to light candles upon the sepulchres of the dead, and hath under him six and twentie legions.

Scot

The scarcity of sources for this spirit matches the two above, making the Weyer line important for preserving details of several spirits currently unknown elsewhere. Bifrons is a Latin title of Janus, though this may not prove an association between the two.

GAMIGIN...

Weyer's spirits	Livre des Esperitz list	Book of Offices 1ˢᵗ list
Gamigin	Cagyne, Cogin	Sogan, Sogom

GAMIGIN, MATHERS' *GOETIA*

Gamigin is a great marquesse, and is seene in the forme of a little horsse, when he taketh humane shape he speaketh with a hoarse voice, disputing of all liberall sciences; he bringeth also to passe, that the soules, which are drowned in the sea, or which dwell in purgatorie (which is called Cartagra, that is, affliction of soules) shall take aierie bodies, and evidentlie appeare and answer to interrogatories at the conjurors commandement; he tarrieth with the exorcist, untill he have accomplished his desire, and hath thirtie legions under him.

Scot

This spirit is another necromantic specialist, although not as difficult to trace in other source texts as others.

ZAGAN...

Weyer's spirits	Book of Offices list one	Book of Offices list two	Livre des Esperitz (list)	Livre des Esperitz (catalog)	Liber de Angelis
Zagam, Zagan	Unidentified	Uriell, Uriall (!)	Zagon (and Dragon, Prince?)	Bugan (King)	Zagam

ZAGAN, MATHERS' GOETIA

Zagan is not apparently mentioned in company with other kings in the closely related texts of Weyer, Scot or the *Goetia*. Nevertheless, casting the net further reveals him as a very major figure. Firstly, concerning him, Scot's text is as follows:

> Zagan is a great king and a president, he commeth abroad like a bull, with griphens wings, but when he taketh humane shape, he maketh men wittie, he turneth all mettals into the coine of that dominion, and turneth water into wine, and wine into water, he also turneth bloud into wine, and wine into bloud, and a foole into a wise man, he is head of thirtie and three legions.

Important to note here are the dual role as King and President. The *Livre des Esperitz* lists him as King Zagon; another unidentified Prince, Dragon, may represent him in his other role. As King Bugan he also appears in its catalogue, while Dragon is omitted.

He has yet to be identified in the first part of the *Book of Offices*, but in the second he is clearly listed under Paimon, King of the West. Another very likely candidate is Uriell aka Uriall, a spirit under Egyn, King of the North. In this case the same attributes of transforming metals and liquids, and making fools wise are supplemented by conferring invisibility. He has a different form, that of a boisterous king, and a hoarse voice. He is the second spirit listed, which in the other columns is an obvious place of prominence. While undoubtedly representing a 'demon' here, the name given is close to identical with that of a major angel. Note that Princes or Presidents in these grimoires have pronounced intermediary status, which is also an attribute of Uriel the angel.

He is very possibly to be identified with Darogan/Itarogan in ToS (recension C), who has 300 legions in common with known kings therein. 'Tarragon' is of course etymologically connected with Dragon. The relevant text is also significant:

> Can clean all trash and make the poor as the wealthy, and wherever he is, he rules.

The *Liber de Angelis* is a C15th book containing numerous magical images and characters (see *Conjuring Spirits*). In it a ritual is given in which Zagam is invoked at a crossroads in an operation of amatory magic. After three days of conjuring him in the same manner, the magician collects an unspecified 'figure' from the crossroads; this I suspect may be either an image or sigil of the spirit. The ritual places Zagan/Zagam in important company, as image-making rituals of a similar kind involving Bael and Belial are known from other such collections. All three of course are Kings in the spirit listings under consideration.

ORIAS...

Weyer's spirits	Others
Orias	Possibly Ornias of the *Testament* and *Hygromanteia*.

ORIAS, MATHERS' GOETIA

Orias is a great marquesse, and is seene as a lion riding on a strong horsse, with a serpents taile, and carrieth in his right hand two great serpents hissing, he knoweth the mansion of planets and perfectlie teacheth the vertues of the starres, he transformeth men, he giveth dignities, prelacies, and confirmations, and also the favour of freends and foes, and hath under him thirtie legions.

Scot

Given the possibility of connecting this spirit with Ornias, it is unfortunate that the main relatives of the Weyer catalogue appear to make no mention of him. The resemblance of the two serpents in his hand to a caduceus is perhaps not accidental, and might indicate some such kind of intermediary role.

VALAC...

Weyer's spirits	Book of Offices 1st list	Others
Valac	Coolor, Doolas	Valac. *clm 849*

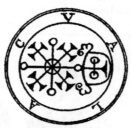

VALAC, MATHERS' GOETIA

Valac is a great president, and commeth abroad with angels wings like a boie, riding on a twoheaded dragon, he perfectlie answereth of treasure hidden, and where serpents may be seene, which he delivereth into the conjurors hands, void of anie force or strength, and hath dominion over thirtie legions of divels.

Scot

The reference to serpents and the possession of thirty legions is shared with the previous spirit. Also, the rank of President might be appropriate to the Orias of the *Testament*. Making such an identification has to remain speculative for the time being.

GOMORY...

Weyer's spirits	Livre des Esperitz (catalog)	Book of Offices list one	Others
Gomory, resembles Paymon	Samon (King, resembles Paymon)	Gemyem. Carmeryn, Cayenam. Gemon	Gaeneron, German Honorius.

Gomory a strong and a mightie duke, he appeareth like a faire woman, with a duchesse crownet about hir midle, riding on a camell, he answereth well and truelie of things present, past, and to come, and of treasure hid, and where it lieth: he procureth the love of women, especiallie of maids, and hath six and twentie legions.

Scot

Gomory is a 'ghost' of Paimon and as such has been referred to previously. The spirit bears the rank of King in the LdE; presumably the 'sub-king' or 'interior' kind of kingship would apply if such duplication has a purpose as hypothesised.

DECARABIA...

Weyer's spirits	Book of Offices list one	Book of Offices List two
Decarabia, Carabia	Possibly Barton, Bartyn	Cambra

DECARABIA, MATHERS' GOETIA

A King or Count in Weyer, ranks are omitted in Scot, while accounted a Marquis in the *Goetia*. As Cambra this spirit is listed under Amaymon in the *Book of Offices*.

> Decarabia or Carabia, he commeth like a * and knoweth the force of herbes and pretious stones, and maketh all birds flie before the exorcist, and to tarrie with him, as though they were tame, and that they shall drinke and sing, as their maner is, and hath thirtie legions.
>
> Scot

The asterisk originally represented a blank or omission in a MS, not a literal star. The *Book of Offices* appropriately and helpfully gives Cambra the form of a swan.

AMDUSCIAS...

Weyer's spirits	Others
Amduscias	Unidentified

AMDUSCIAS, FROM JACQUES COLLIN DE PLANCY'S *DICTIONNAIRE INFERNAL*

AMDUSIAS, MATHERS' *GOETIA*

Amduscias a great and a strong duke, he commeth foorth as an unicorne, when he standeth before his maister in humane shape, being commanded, he easilie bringeth to passe, that trumpets and all musicall instruments may be heard and not seene, and also that trees shall bend and incline, according to the conjurors will, he is excellent among familiars, and hath nine and twentie legions.

Scot

ANDRAS...

Weyer's spirits	Others
Andras	Unidentified

ANDRAS, FROM JACQUES COLLIN DE PLANCY'S *DICTIONNAIRE INFERNAL*

ANDRAS, MATHERS' *GOETIA*

Andras is a great marquesse, and is seene in an angels shape with a head like a blacke night raven, riding upon a blacke and a verie strong woolfe, flourishing with a sharpe sword in his hand, he can kill the maister, the servant, and all assistants, he is author of discords, and ruleth thirtie legions.

Scot

Quite possibly Andaras in the *ms. Plut.89 Sup.38.*

World spirits		Others	
Angels		Dark allies	

Andras is a great marquis, and appeareth in an angels shape with a head like a black night raven, riding upon a black and very strong wolfe, flourishing with a sharpe sword in his hand, he can kill the master, the servant, and all accessaries, he is author of discords, and ruleth thirty legions.

—Scot

Little possible Andras in these ap. Plate 89 and 98

COMPARISONS: PART FOUR

WEYER REMAINDER (1) = *LIVRE DES ESPERITZ*

Weyer	Rank	*Livre des Esperitz* (list)	*Livre des Esperitz* (catalog)
Androalphus, Andrealphus	Marquis	Andralfas	Tudiras Hoho
Oze (Ose)	President	Ose	Ose (marquis)
Aym, Haborym	Duke		
Orobas	Prince		
Vapula	Duke		
Cimeries	Marquis		(Marquis Tvueries in *clm 849*)
Amy	President		(President Hanni in *clm 849*)
Flauros	Duke	Flanos	Flavos
Balam	King		
Alocer, Allocer	Duke		
Zaleos, Saleos	Earl		
Wal, Vuall	Duke		
Haagenti	President		
Phoenix	Marquis	Fenix	Fenix
Stolas	Prince	Distolas	Distolas

WEYER REMAINDER (2) = BOOK OF OFFICES. GERMAN HONORIUS.

Weyer	Book of Offices list one	Book of Offices list two	Others
Androalphus, Andrealphus			
Oze (Ose)		Oze	
Aym, Haborym		Pathyn	
Orobas			
Vapula	Similar to Moyle		
Cimeries			clm 849 Tvueries
Amy			clm 849 Hanni
Flauros			
Balam (Abelam)	Baasan	Barson (heads differ)	
Alocer, Allocer	Boal, Boall is very similar	Lechor	
Zaleos, Saleos		Caleos	
Wal, Vuall		Reyall	
Haagenti (duplicates Zagan)			
Phoenix			
Stolas		Mistolas	
			Marquis Lucay, Ducay LdE, Marquis Sucax clm 849 Suchay in Offices.

ANDREALPHUS...

Weyer's spirits	*Livre des Esperitz* (list)	*Livre des Esperitz* (catalog)
Andrealphus	Andralfus	Tudiras Hoho

ANDREALPHUS, MATHERS' GOETIA

Andrealphus is a great marquesse, appearing as a pecocke, he raiseth great noises, and in humane shape perfectlie teacheth geometrie, and all things belonging to admeasurements, he maketh a man to be a subtill disputer, and cunning in astronomie, and transformeth a man into the likenes of a bird, and there are under him thirtie legions.

Scot

'Tu diras' is a Spanish phrase meaning 'you decide'; an editor's remark or in-joke is, of course, likelier than an alias.

OSE...

Weyer's spirits	Livre des Esperitz (list)	Livre des Esperitz (catalog)	Book of Offices list two
Ose	Oze	Ose	Oze

Ose is a great president, and commeth foorth like a leopard, and counterfeting to be a man, he maketh one cunning in the liberall sciences, he answereth truelie of divine and secret things, he transformeth a mans shape, and bringeth a man to that madnes, that he thinketh himselfe to be that which he is not; as that he is a king or a pope, or that he weareth a crowne on his head, Durátque id regnum ad horam.

Scot

Offices has Oze in the Southern column.

AYM/HABORYM...

Weyer's spirits	Book of Offices list two
Aym/Haborym	Pathyn

AYM, MATHERS' GOETIA

Aym or Haborim is a great duke and a strong, he commeth foorth with three heads, the first like a serpent, the second like a man having two * the third like a cat, he rideth on a viper, carrieng in his hand a light fier brand, with the flame whereof castels and cities are fiered, he maketh one wittie everie kind of waie, he answereth truelie of privie matters, and reigneth over twentie six legions.

Scot

Offices' Pathyn is in the Southern column. The asterisk here, as usual, represents a gap in the text; I strongly suspect 'horns' was the original reading.

OROBAS...

Weyer's spirits	Others
Orobas	Unidentified

OROBAS, FROM JACQUES COLLIN DE PLANCY'S *DICTIONNAIRE INFERNAL*

OROBAS, MATHERS' *GOETIA*

Orobas is a great prince, he commeth foorth like a horsse, but when he putteth on him a mans idol, he talketh of divine vertue, he giveth true answers of things present, past, and to come, and of the divinitie, and of the creation, he deceiveth none, nor suffereth anie to be tempted, he giveth dignities and prelacies, and the favour of freends and foes, and hath rule over twentie legions.

Scot

Seemingly Orobas is unknown, at least under this name, outside of Weyer's spirit list.

VAPULA...

Weyer's spirits	Others
Vapula	Unidentified

VAPULA, MATHERS' GOETIA

Vapula is a great duke and a strong, he is seene like a lion with griphens wings, he maketh a man subtill and wonderfull in handicrafts, philosophie, and in sciences conteined in bookes, and is ruler over thirtie six legions.

Scot

There are similarities between Vapula and *Oberon*'s Moyle (1st list); I prefer to err on the side of caution here.

CIMERIES...

Weyer's spirits	Book of Offices list one	Others
Cimeries	Sowrges	Tvueries, *clm 849*

Cimeries is a great marquesse and a strong, ruling in the parts of Aphrica; he teacheth perfectlie grammar, logicke, and rhetorike, he discovereth treasures and things hidden, he bringeth to passe, that a man shall seeme with expedition to be turned into a soldier, he rideth upon a great blacke horsse, and ruleth twentie legions.

Scot

His rulership in parts of Africa is an important factor, and may point to connections with high ranking spirits. Geographical rulerships as a one-time feature of the catalogues is less pronounced in the Weyer stemma, but – like image making – undoubtedly connect with the spirit hierarchy in some former presentations. Also see earlier remarks about the likely equal status of Marquises and Dukes, and their rule of different times of day.

AMY...

Weyer's spirits	Book of Offices list one	Book of Offices list two	Others
Amy	Hanar, also Tamor/Chamor	Gamor	Hanni, *clm 849*

AMY, MATHERS' GOETIA

Amy is a great president, and appeareth in a flame of fier, but having taken mans shape, he maketh one marvelous in astrologie, and in all the liberall sciences, he procureth excellent familiars, he bewraieth treasures preserved by spirits, he hath the governement of thirtie six legions, he is partlie of the order of angels, partlie of potestats, he hopeth after a thousand two hundreth yeares to returne to the seventh throne: which is not credible.

Scot

It is tempting to wonder if the 'which is not credible' represents a disapproving editorial comment. Pro-Origen elements in the grimoire in an earlier form are a tantalising prospect; he is certainly mentioned with approval in the *GoS*. Gamor is under the southern rule of Amamymon in *Off*.

FLAUROS...

Weyer's spirits	Livre des Esperitz (list)
Flauros	Flanos

FLAUROS, FROM JACQUES COLLIN DE PLANCY'S *DICTIONNAIRE INFERNAL*

Flauros a strong duke, is seene in the forme of a terrible strong leopard, in humane shape, he sheweth a terrible countenance, and fierie eies, he answereth trulie and fullie of things present, past, and to come; if he be in a triangle, he lieth in all things and deceiveth in other things, and beguileth in other busines, he gladlie talketh of the divinitie, and of the creation of the world, and of the fall; he is constrained by divine vertue, and so are all divels or spirits, to burne and destroie all the conjurors adversaries. And if he be commanded, he suffereth the conjuror not to be tempted, and he hath twentie legions under him.

Scot

Not so far identified in *Oberon/Offices*, linkages with the god Horus should, reluctantly, be taken with a pinch of salt. The Triangle of Solomon is mentioned here again. Its purpose of enforcing truthfulness – rather than assisting manifestation as modern sources frequently allege – is apparent when comparing these references.

BALAM...

Weyer's spirits	Book of Offices list two
Balam (Abelam)	Barson (heads differ)

BALAN, FROM JACQUES COLLIN DE PLANCY'S *DICTIONNAIRE INFERNAL*

BALAM, MATHERS' *GOETIA*

Balam is a great and a terrible king, he commeth foorth with three heads, the first of a bull, the second of a man, the third of a ram, he hath a serpents taile, and flaming eies, riding upon a furious beare, and carrieng a hawke on his fist, he speaketh with

Pandemonium: A Discordant Concordance of Diverse Spirit Catalogues

a hoarse voice, answering perfectlie of things present, past, and
to come, hee maketh a man invisible and wise, hee governeth
fourtie legions, and was of the order of dominations.

Scot

King Balam is one of the success stories of a comparative approach to
the spirit catalogues. Often supposed to be related to a biblical sorcerer
due to what may be an accidental resemblance of his name in the *Goetia*,
he has various names in different grimoires, and occasionally in the same
one. By comparing Weyer's Long Text concerning Paimon with the *Book
of Offices* matters become clear. In the appropriate Long Text Paimon has
two subordinate kings, Abelam and Belial, In *Offices'* account of Paimon
two kings are mentioned, Barson and Belial. The description of Barson
differs slightly from the Weyer version of Balam, but it is clear we are
dealing with the same spirit: Abelam aka Balam aka Barson (Bason in
Campbell's text). This shows the fluidity of the spelling, and should wean
us off assuming a possibly erroneous association with biblical Balaam.

However, the trail does not finish there, and nor do the variants on
the name. This is an important spirit, and can probably be identified
in various 'stand alone' rituals appearing in several key texts. Firstly, I
postulate that Barson is to be identified with the spirit Baron.

Staying initially with the *Book of Oberon*, Baron is present in various
parts of the work. He appears first (p114) in connection with magical
characters for his ritual. In the footnotes the editors inform us that Baron
is given as 'Barachin' and 'Baraham or Baron' in parallel forms of this text
(*Wellcome MS110, 39v* and *Sloane 3853. 215r* respectively). On p115 he is
described as good for hidden treasure, which differs from usual accounts
of Balam. It is a major concern however, of magicians – the spirits of
each day of the week in *Honorius* have treasure hunting as a given. Most
likely this power was a major reason for conjuring various spirits and
could thus be grafted onto their descriptions. The text mentions without
specifying that he is 'able to do many other things', so it is clear where
the author's interest lies. In short this account of Baron's powers may be
abbreviated but is nonetheless fairly routine.

Of more interest are some additional hands on remarks on the ritual
process and in particular the last; I summarise them here. He may be

conjured on any day and in any hour, day or night, in the bedroom, out in a field, alone or with two or three companions, but alone is preferred. A magical circle is to be 'made in the earth'. Then, importantly 'but once you have spoken with the spirit once within the circle you will not need it again'.

This is identical to my own practice, and I interpret the characters' purpose with the use of characters in the GV on that basis. In other words, full ceremonial the first time, in which an agreement is reached employing the magical characters; thereafter contact is made via a simpler agreed formula.

Next, on p347 is given a conjuration of Baron, described as the 'first northern spirit'. We would do well not to place too great an emphasis on the particular direction mentioned, but that he is an important directional king supports the identity with Balam. Note in addition that the *Book of Treasure Spirits* (*Sloane MS 3825*) gives a ritual where Vassago swears by his king 'Baro the king of the West'. This is more in accord with the classic version of Paimon and her ministers. On the other hand, *Offices* also gives Vassago as northern, one of the few clearly identifiable figures under Egyn.

On p426 more variants on the name appear; Baron, Baaran, Bareth, or Baryth. These variants require considering possible connections between Baron and Berith rather than Balam. Though a necessary question, Berith's appearance and powers are very different and the two should be distinguished clearly. Here too we are told – as in the account just mentioned – that Baron can be conjured at any time, and, within limits, at any convenient place. A different form of characters is used, but the process is essentially similar. The account of his powers here is closer to Balam; he can tell you anything you wish, as Balam can answer anything past, present, or future. Baron also has the power of transportation, which for practical reasons among others is common with treasure spirits.

Possible duplicates in *Book of Offices* include list 1 34 Barton, a duke like a bear with dragon tail, expert in herbs/stones, can carry you from region to region, with 30 legions, who is definitely duplicated in 38 Bartyn, bear, herbs/stones, also a carrier with 20 legions, and possibly 69 Bartax, a ruler.

In *Book of Offices*, list 2, our Barson is identified as a King under Paimon who makes invisible and wise, and who has three heads. There is every reason to consider Barson an aka of Balam. Is he also Baron? I leave it for the reader to decide.

Incidentally, Scot's Bealphares, like Baron, can be called 'at any time', excels in carrying (and finding) hidden treasure, and also requires characters not unlike operations of Baron. His ritual directly follows Baron's in the *Grimoire of Arthur Gauntlet*. This, of course, demonstrates similar considerations in composition, not identity. In *Oberon* Bealphares is mentioned in a note below the 2nd spirit list. His relevance to this spirit hierarchy as a wider topic is likely in my opinion.

ALLOCER...

Weyer's spirits	*Book of Offices* list two
Alocer, Allocer	Lechor

ALOCER, FROM JACQUES COLLIN DE PLANCY'S *DICTIONNAIRE INFERNAL*

ALLOCES, MATHERS' *GOETIA*

Allocer is a strong duke and a great, he commeth foorth like a soldier, riding on a great horsse, he hath a lions face, verie red, and with flaming eies, he speaketh with a big voice, he maketh a man woonderfull in astronomie, and in all the liberall sciences, he bringeth good familiars, and ruleth thirtie six legions.

Scot

The only apparent 'Prelate' in the literature, namely Boal or Boall in *Oberon*, is very similar in appearance, but with different powers. That Prelates may represent an entirely different class of spirit – absent in the *Goetia* as generally understood – militates against identifying them as one spirit. Lechor is under Paymon according to *Offices* 2nd list.

SALEOS...

Weyer's spirits	*Book of Offices* list two
Saleos	Caleos

ZAEBOS, FROM JACQUES COLLIN DE PLANCY'S *DICTIONNAIRE INFERNAL*

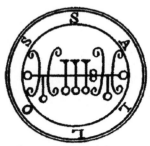

SALLOS, MATHERS' *GOETIA*

Saleos is a great earle, he appeareth as a gallant soldier, riding on a crocodile, and weareth a dukes crowne, peaceable, etc.

Scot

The 'etc' is unusual, and there has obviously been considerable abbreviation by a compiling editor here. It is present in Weyer and doubtless frustrated the translator of Scot's English text. Caleos is under Paymon in *Offices/Oberon*, where more details are forthcoming. Caleos has power and knowledge of 'infinite' treasure. He makes beloved, he also 'purchaseth familiarity'. The latter together might be rendered 'love and favour', but something else may be implied by 'purchaseth'. The description gives both cockatrice and crocodile as possible mounts, and the familiar 'two crowns' which I suspect were originally horns. While Weyer's text calls him 'peaceable', *Oberon* suggests he is not inclined to be truthful without constraint. No legions are mentioned in this part of *Oberon*'s listing, but such details are rarely consistent anyway.

VUALL...

Weyer's spirits	Book of Offices list one
Vuall/Wal	Reyall

VUAL, MATHERS' GOETIA

Vuall is a great duke and a strong, he is seene as a great and terrible dromedarie, but in humane forme, he soundeth out in a base voice the Ægyptian toong. This man above all other procureth the especiall love of women, and knoweth things present, past, and to come, procuring the love of freends and foes, he was of the order of potestats, and governeth thirtie seven legions.

Scot

Reyall is also under Paymon as with the above spirits. This may explain the presence of the dromedary and the speaking of Egyptian. It is not necessary to consider this a duplication; subordinates frequently act in the stead of their superiors in some conceptions of the practicalities, and might share identifying features.

Pandemonium: A Discordant Concordance of Diverse Spirit Catalogues

HAAGENTI...

Weyer's spirits	Others
Haagenti	Unidentified

HAAGENTI, MATHERS' GOETIA

Haagenti is a great president, appearing like a great bull, having the wings of a griphen, but when he taketh humane shape, he maketh a man wise in everie thing, he changeth all mettals into gold, and changeth wine and water the one into the other, and commandeth as manie legions as Zagan.

Scot

The last phrase is extremely telling; it is doubtless an editorial interpolation, possibly by Weyer. In fact, President Haagenti duplicates King Zagam aka Zagan in Weyer, Scot and the *Goetia*. The appearance, powers, and numbers of legions are identical; only the rank differs. No such duplication is apparent in the *Book of Offices* or *Livre de Esperitz*. For practical purposes, both Kings and Presidents attend on a Great King and have important intermediary roles. Meanwhile, Weyer probably would not have understood 'ghosting' in these texts, and was undoubtedly a hostile witness.

PHOENIX...

Weyer's spirits	Livre des Esperitz (list)	Livre des Esperitz (catalog)
Phoenix	Fenix	Fenix

PHENEX, MATHERS' GOETIA

Phoenix is a great marquesse, appearing like the bird Phoenix, having a childs voice: but before he standeth still before the conjuror, he singeth manie sweet notes. Then the exorcist with his companions must beware he give no eare to the melodie, but must by and by bid him put on humane shape; then will he speake marvellouslie of all woonderfull sciences. He is an excellent poet, and obedient, he hopeth to returne to the seventh throne after a thousand two hundreth yeares, and governeth twentie legions.

Scot

Note there is no requirement for the Triangle here, any danger being overcome simply by having the spirit adopt human shape.

STOLAS...

Weyer's spirits	Livre des Esperitz (list)	Livre des Esperitz (catalog)	Book of Offices list two
Stolas	Distolas	Distolas	Mistolas

STOLAS, FROM JACQUES COLLIN DE PLANCY'S *DICTIONNAIRE INFERNAL*

STOLAS, MATHERS' *GOETIA*

Stolas is a great prince, appearing in the forme of a nightraven, before the exorcist, he taketh the image and shape of a man, and teacheth astronomie, absolutelie understanding the vertues of herbes and pretious stones; there are under him twentie six legions.

Scot

Mistolas is a spirit under Paymon in *Offices/Oberon*. Note that Stolas abbreviates the alternative forms; there really are no grounds for preferring Weyer's spellings.

Appendix I

The Other Magicians and the Grimoires

WHEN IT COMES to the grimoires it is very easy to assume they tell the whole story, and that threatening 'evil' spirits with knives and torture was how everyone did it back then. In fact, it is too easy, and almost certainly completely wrong.

The grimoires are the literary tip of an iceberg, whose submerged portion may well have been very different. Also the grimoires – most of which are later than the medieval period – reflect magic during its decline, rather than its heyday. As a comparison, historians point out that astrologers writing in the 1700s were aware their art was becoming sidelined by new tendencies in Western culture.

Stuff starts to happen under these conditions, one of which is gentlemen start to collect grimoires, and the versions produced for them are influenced by the customers. Example: the sword gets more and more prominent in this period, when gentlemen carried them, but is missing entirely from many of the older manuscripts. It is also important to bear in mind that many of the 'aristocratic' manuscripts postdate the printing press by a considerable margin.

There are traces of the 'submerged' part of the tradition here and there in the grimoires. For example, the first book of the *Key of Solomon* has many descriptions of conjuring with knife in hand, but the very last chapter of Book II (Chapter XXII) describes the method of making offerings to the spirits, and has a much more amenable tone. This resembles some of the procedures in the *Picatrix*.

There are also references in the grimoires to how 'others' do things, which indicate that there were practitioners with a different approach around. In the compilation of magical writings found in Scot's *Discoverie of Witchcraft* occurs an interesting passage involving two kinds of practitioner:

Of Magical Circles, and the reason of their Institution.

> Magitians, and the more learned sort of conjurers, make use
> of Circles in various manners, and to various intentions. First,
> when convenience serves not, as to time or place that a real
> Circle should be delineated, they frame an imaginary Circle, by
> means of Incantations and Consecrations, without either Knife,
> Pensil, or Compasses, circumscribing nine foot of ground round
> about them, which they pretend to sanctifie with words and
> Ceremonies, spattering their Holy Water all about so far as the
> said Limit extendeth; and with a form of Consecration following,
> do alter the property of the ground, that from common (as they
> say) it becomes sanctifi'd, and made fit for Magicall uses.

Here clearly the author distinguishes magicians from 'others', among
whom the more learned sort made use of similar materials. Some among
these others were also using the grimoires, and possibly on occasion even
writing them. A contemporary of Dee's, known as Conjuring Minterne,
is a historical example of a 'more learned sort of conjurer' as described
here. A member of the local gentry and resident in a sizeable house,
he was nevertheless closer to the cunning folk in orientation. However,
identifying a social distinction between historical persons does not go far
enough. It is mechanistic and by failing mythology distorts history, and
that way lies Murrayism. So let us dig deeper.

Another such reference occurs in the *Goetia of Solomon* describing a
particular spirit:

> Berith is a great and terrible Duke, and hath three names. Of
> some he is called Beall; of the Jews Berith; of Necromancers
> Bolfry.

Here, plainly (since he uses the name Berith himself), the
author or compositor is distinguishing what he does and approves
of from the methodology of another group of magicians. Who
were these 'others'? It is fairly natural, given the context and
other indicators, to assume that the approach of the text is close to

the attitudes of 'the Jews' and further from 'the Necromancers', leaving 'some' completely unaccounted for. It would be interesting to know who Michael Scot was describing in his writings on magic, as potential candidates for historical models. Meanwhile, other indications suggest the 'some' and 'the Necromancers' may well have used offerings over threats in their approach. There is no indication they did things the same way, and traces of these 'other ways' are still around.

Immediately before the offerings chapter in *KOS* we get a chapter on preparing the Book of Spirits. There is some ambiguity here, as the *Key of Solomon* version seems to be about a book with planetary angels in it, give or take a reference to 'spirits'. Yet almost everywhere else in the grimoires the impression one gets of the 'Book of Spirits' is that it is far more likely to contain names of 'demons'; is Solomon being dishonest, or merely coy?

The *4th Book* is much more forthcoming; it says first that methods of making such a 'Book of Spirits' are 'extant among those magicians who do most use the ministry of evil spirits'. This certainly either makes Solomon look a little less than honest, or indicates that contemporary opinions about the spirits were a little less cut and dried – take your pick. It then gives two approaches to making the Book of Spirits (the first is much like Solomon) suggesting Agrippa knew of texts just like the *Key*, but also knew more.

The second approach described by Agrippa is quite different. It involves action at a crossroads, and is closer to other traditions, including 'New World' traditions and the much earlier rites of the papyri. It also resembles later French sources (*The Cabala of the Black Pullet* not least of all). Was this method – or something like it – the one preferred by 'others' or by 'Nigromancers'? Why does the *Key* not mention it? Why does the *Key* pretend this book of spirits' is about planetary angels (bearing in mind that much earlier Solomonic works mention planetary demons)? Has the *Liber Spirituum* been 'cleaned up', after learned appropriation?

Wellcome MS 4666 meanwhile gives an account of Leviathan, describing him as extremely formidable. The magician will require powerful conjurations, being brave, firm, and bold from within the confines of the Circle. However, it goes on to mention that he carries Witches who have made a pact with him to the Sabbat. Plainly being carried by Leviathan indicates the absence of a Circle in these journeys. The MS also tells us he can bestow powders, unguents, and familiars, all of which were fairly typical of witchcraft as then understood. So what we see here is a 'status quo' magician trying to appropriate unto himself the gifts these spirits freely bestowed on their intimates. The next spirit in the MS is Berith, interestingly enough. Here's another from the same text.

> Nambroth: aka Frimost, among a great many interesting details we learn that he 'attends the nocturnal assemblies of the Lebanese'. Presumably a 'heretical' sect is intended, such as the Druze – again the implication is that this spirit does not 'belong' to the grimoirists, he is part of someone else's pantheon.

Elsewhere, under Gaap, Weyer's text has this to say:

> There were certain necromancers that offered sacrifices and burnt offerings unto him; and to call him up, they exercised an art, saying that Solomon the wise made it. Which is false: for it was rather Cham, the sonne of Noah, who after the floud began first to invocate wicked spirits...

These indications are not infrequent in the old literature. Whatever the reality of the case, the understanding plainly existed that the spirits 'Solomonic' grimoirists attempted to compel were simultaneously invoked and regarded quite differently by some other sect or group. While historical cunning folk account for some of these 'others', we are also walking here in mythological territory. Witches and heretics as portrayed in Roman literature and Christian polemics – portrayals melding with popular belief and influencing magical writings – are as much occupants of this space as the spirits. In other words, the others, like the spirits, are subjects of belief.

As beliefs, this is a natural progression from the *Testament of Solomon* and early Christianity, in which figures of pagan belief were identified with demons. In the grimoire conception, the witch and the demon are companions at the Sabbat while the cleric represents the opposition. As a precedent, there are obvious implications for modern practice.

Plainly it was to these 'others' that the spirits more truly 'belonged' and vice versa. Moreover, this understanding partly explains the coercive element of grimoire practice. Whether the relationship of these spirits as named with heretics and witches is factual or not is not wholly relevant, or important. 'Mythologically' they belong to those practicing forbidden magic, which is to say goetia. The practitioners of this 'other' magic are identified as necromancers, appropriately as shown in the *Encyclopaedia Goetica*. While their otherness as mythological figures does not involve paganism as a quantifiable sociological identity, it is nevertheless wholly characteristic. The other magicians occupy the same outside space as the spirits: pagan, heretical, and diabolical. They are of course also utterly essential to the conceptual universe of would-be 'establishment' magicians.

This is partway to explaining why the *Goetia of Solomon* is so curiously named. The author is associating the spirits, rather than the magic, with goetia. This is a kind of get-out clause: 'it's not me who is into black magic, it's the spirits'. Therefore, by its own lights and despite confusion resulting from the title, the GoS is not goetic, the spirits are. This is at least partly nonsense, since goetia means 'witchcraft, magic, sorcery' – calling the GoS spirits 'Goetias' or 'Goetics' produces only a semantic tangle. Goetia is something you do; such spirits as named above are who you do it with.

The other magicians are identified as authentic by their mythological otherness. True ritual is a wholly mythological process; the mechanics of ritual and the syntax of myth are so close at points as to be identical. The magician must at least be able to visit mythological space, if not abide there, rather than simply attempt to fearfully exploit it.

The grimoires are monuments of what may be called magic's 'interim period'. They are disfigured by a dualism which was not originally native to goetic tradition, but entered via the backdoor of changes in religion. Recognising Otherness as a characteristic magicians share with spirits enables us to surmount this abiding difficulty in Western magic. So again, departure from the grimoires, particularly the routine employment of coercive elements and dualistic models, is not a break with tradition, it is a return.

Appendix II

List of Tables

BIBLIOGRAPHY AND FURTHER READING

Betz, Hans Dieter (ed.): *The Greek Magical Papyri in Translation*. University of Chicago Press. 1986. 2nd edition 1992.

Campbell, Colin D, (ed): *A Book of the Offices of Spirits*. Teitan Press. York Beach USA. 2011.

Davidson, Gustav: *A Dictionary of Angels*. The Free Press. New York. 1967.

Davies, Owen: Grimoires: *A History of Magic Books*. Oxford University Press. 2009.

Fanger, Claire (ed.): *Conjuring Spirits*. Sutton Publishing Limited. UK. 1998.

Kieckhefer, Richard: *Forbidden Rites, a Necromancer's Manual of the Fifteenth Century*. Pennsylvania State Press. Pennsylvania USA. 1997.

Leitch, Aaron: *Secrets of the Magical Grimoires*. Llewellyn. Minnesota. 2005.

Lecouteux, Claude: (English edition). *The Book of Grimoires*. Inner Traditions. Toronto. 2013.

Maggi, Humberto: *Daemonology; an Introduction with a Selection of Texts*. Hadean Press. West Yorkshire. 2015.

Marakathis, Ioannis (ed): *The Magical Treatise of Solomon, or Hygromanteia*. Golden Hoard Publishing. Singapore. 2011.

Rankine, David: *The Book of Treasure Spirits*. Avalonia. 2009.
: *The Grimoire of Arthur Gauntlet*. Avalonia. 2011.

Rankine, David and Barron, Paul Harry (ed): *The Complete Grimoire of Pope Honorius*. Avalonia. 2013.

Peterson, Joseph (ed): *The Lesser Key of Solomon*. Weiser. York Beach USA. 2001.
: *Grimorium Verum*. CreateSpace Publishing. California. USA. 2007.

with Harms, Daniel and Clark, James R.: *The Book of Oberon*. Llewellyn. Minnesota. USA. 2015.

Scot, Reginald: *The Discoverie of Witchcraft* (various editions).

Skinner, Steve and Rankine, David (ed): *The Keys to the Gateway of Magic*. Golden Hoard. Singapore. 2011.
: *The Veritable Keys of Solomon*. Llewellyn. Minnesota USA. 2008.

Stratton-Kent, Jake: *An Inventorie of Demons*. Hadean Press. 2016.
A Prince among Spirits. Hadean Press. 2016.
Frimost and Klepoth. Hadean Press. 2011.
The Testament of Cyprian the Mage. Scarlet Imprint. 2014.
The True Grimoire. Scarlet Imprint. 2010.

Young, Francis (trans.): *The Cambridge Book of Magic*. Cambridge. 2015.

Index

A

R

S

Tuesday 37, 38

U

Um 53
Underworld Sun 34
Uriell 203
Ursa Major 49

V

Valac
  main entry 205
Valefar
  main entry 105
Valefor 41
Vapula
  main entry 217
Vassago 53, 54, 224
Vepar
  main entry 178
Vine
  main entry 199
Vuall
  main entry 230

W

Wednesday 38, 40, 92
West 70, 101, 140, 150, 153, 156, 202
Weyer 69, 72, 117

Z

Zagam 231
Zagan
  main entry 202–203
Zagon. *See* Zagan
Zayme 196
Zepar 178
  main entry 145
Zimimar 72
Zoray 41

Lightning Source UK Ltd.
Milton Keynes UK
UKOW06f0812050117
291430UK00002B/187/P